# Own Your Career

## Take Charge, Build Momentum, and Shape Your Future

# Own Your Career

## Take Charge, Build Momentum, and Shape Your Future

### R. D. BENNETT

# Contents

"

*Without Goals, and Plans to Reach Them,*
*You Are Like a Ship That Has Set Sail*
*with No Destination."*

— **Fitzhugh Dodson**

# 1

# Introduction

Over a lifetime, the average person spends approximately 90,000 hours, or about 13 years, working. Given how large a portion of our lives this represents, career choices can have a profound impact on our happiness, health, and financial security. Career growth, long-term vision, and workplace culture are not just professional considerations; they are life-shaping decisions.

When considering your career, it's important to reflect on your needs, priorities, and long-term hopes. Before anything else, ask yourself whether you are looking for a job or a career. A job primarily focuses on earning an income, often without contributing to long-term professional development or commitment. While a career is a long-term professional journey made up of multiple roles, shaped by purpose, growth, and goals that are developed over time.

For those of you just starting out, the first step is identifying the field in which you want to build a career. In 2024, Gallup partnered with the Amazon Future Engineer program in the UK, France, and Germany to examine career interests among 15-year-old students. Using data from the Programme for International Student Assessment (PISA), part of the

Organisation for Economic Co-operation and Development (OECD), the study found that at least four in ten students in each country could not envision what career they might have by age 30. This uncertainty highlights how difficult career planning can be, even early on.

When embarking on a career, it's essential to research both the work itself and the typical career path to fully understand what will truly be involved. There is little value in spending years training to become a surgeon if you don't like the sight of blood. While extreme, this example illustrates a broader point: what sounds appealing in theory may not work in practice. Be honest with yourself about your likes and dislikes, strengths and weaknesses, and the long-term opportunities and areas for growth within your chosen field.

For those who have already chosen a career path, the journey may already be underway. You may have a destination in mind, but have you mapped out the route? When was the last time you truly evaluated where you are and where you want to go? Once you enter the workforce, it's easy to get swept up in deadlines, projects, and targets. However, it's equally important to step back periodically and assess whether your current trajectory still aligns with your goals.

Every new skill and experience you gain adds depth to your professional profile and can help speed up your career. When setbacks occur, whether through layoffs, roles that don't meet expectations, or unforeseen challenges, try to reframe them as part of your broader career journey. Setbacks are inevitable, but they don't define you. When you go off track, fall behind, or make mistakes, you often gain valuable layers of experience that you can use as leverage later.

There is no single "better" career path, only the one that fits your goals and timing. While a few individuals climb the corporate ladder within a single organization to the highest levels, they are the exception rather than the rule. In most industries, demonstrated experience matters, and growth often comes from continuously challenging yourself through new roles and responsibilities.

If your employer has outlined career pathways, review them carefully and with curiosity. In some organizations, they design these paths primarily around business needs rather than individual development. There is nothing inherently wrong with this; when a company invests in you, it expects a return, whether through time, expertise, or institutional knowledge. Ultimately, however, companies act in their own best interests. That is the nature of business.

This book is about taking ownership of your career. It aims to help you define your professional direction, identify skills that support long-term growth, and recognize pitfalls that can stall progress. The goal is to equip you with the tools to shape a career that benefits you, not just in the short term, but over the course of your working life.

A useful way to think about your career is to view yourself as a company, and you are the product. Which market do you want to operate in? How will you differentiate yourself? You, as CEO of *You Inc.*, need to get the best return possible from investing in yourself. Consider how best to use your resources, build longevity, and increase earning potential. Is your career moving in the right direction, or do you see potential obstacles ahead? Approaching your career with this mindset allows you to plan strategically and decide based on long-term value rather than emotion alone.

Emotions often keep us stuck in roles longer than is beneficial. Fear of change can lead to rationalizations such as:

- The money is good
- The people are okay
- The grass isn't always greener
- It's convenient
- I have flexibility
- I'm comfortable

While these factors may contribute to short-term satisfaction, they can also limit professional growth. The skills you're developing now may benefit your employer more than they benefit you. If your role disappears, you might find that your expertise, perfect for your current job, is now outdated or hard to transfer.

The benefits of staying with one employer for an entire career have diminished significantly. People used to view job hopping negatively but now see it as an accepted reality when done strategically. Today, "Why did you stay?" can be just as common as "Why did you leave?" That said, it's important to distinguish between short, frequent moves that raise concerns and deliberate career transitions made for growth. In January 2022, U.S. Census Bureau data showed that 34% of workers had been with their employer for less than three years, compared with 27% who had been with their employer for ten years or more.

Compensation is another important consideration. Changing roles can accelerate salary growth, while staying may allow benefits and leadership opportunities to compound. Often, the most effective strategy blends both approaches: move when growth stalls, stay when opportunities align.

Market conditions also matter. Pew Research found that between April 2021 and March 2022, 60% of workers who switched employers experienced an increase in real earnings, with half seeing gains of 9.7% or more. During the same period, the median worker who stayed experienced a 1.7% loss. However, this was during an unusually hot labor market. More recent data from the Federal Reserve Bank of Atlanta shows that between February and July 2025, wage growth for job stayers slightly outpaced that of job switchers (4.1% versus 4%). In strong markets, job hopping pays; in weaker markets, stability may be safer. The economic environment therefore matters.

Beyond money, consider what you truly want from your career. Not everyone aspires to become a CEO. Some people prefer technical mastery to people management. The traditional linear path, from individual contributor to manager, director, vice president, and executive, does not reflect most modern careers. Real careers have layers, detours, and sidesteps. Skills multiply rather than simply add up, and knowledge compounds in unexpected ways. Your knowledge and abilities determine your experience.

You should periodically reassess your career goals. What works when you're 18 years old may not work at age 30, and what worked at age 30 may not fit at age 55. Life circumstances, priorities, and interests can change. A career that once felt like the perfect match may no longer align with who you are or what you want.

This book helps you navigate the career ladder, optimize your strengths, and position yourself to take advantage of opportunities. It also highlights behaviors and patterns that can stall progress or derail growth entirely. These strategies come from my experience and the experience of other professionals. What once worked no longer applies in the same way. Staying with one employer for an entire career is increasingly rare, and employers don't always show loyalty back. Companies must evolve to survive, and employees must do the same to remain relevant.

There will be bumps along the way. You will encounter supportive, mediocre, and toxic managers. Hopefully, you'll have more highs than lows, experiencing both. You may settle somewhere for a time and feel you've found your professional "home." Still, it's important to remain aware, curious, and open to change. Comfort can quietly stall a career.

Organizations change. Leadership changes. Priorities shift. Over time, people may forget your long hours and sacrifices. Recognizing this isn't cynical; it's realistic. Your career belongs to you, not your employer. So, build it intentionally. Treat it as your own enterprise. Climb the ladder to the level that suits you, in the direction you choose, and step off only when *you* decide.

"*Begin With the End in Mind.*"

— **Stephen Covey**

# 2

# Defining Your Career Vision and Creating Your Roadmap

Your career begins with clarity, clarity about what you want, what matters to you, and where you ultimately want to go. Whether you are just starting out or considering your next chapter, taking time to define your vision gives you a sense of direction and purpose. From there, you can translate that vision into practical, achievable goals and build a roadmap that guides your journey step by step.

This chapter brings together the two most important building blocks of career growth:

(1) Understanding your long-term vision, and
(2) Turning that vision into a structured roadmap you can follow

## Understanding Your Career Vision

Before you plan your next move, pause and look at the bigger picture. Ask yourself:

- What kind of work energizes me?
- What drains me?
- What does success look like in my life, not someone else's?
- What do I value most: stability, creativity, impact, learning, financial growth, or flexibility?
- What roles match not just my skill set, but my personality and interests?

This is the time to be honest with yourself. Trying to meet expectations set by others often leads to burnout or dissatisfaction. Your vision should reflect your strengths, values, and long-term aspirations, not the path someone else believes you "should" take.

It can be helpful to talk your thoughts through with someone objective, a mentor, colleague, or friend who has no stake in your decisions. An outside perspective often clarifies what you enjoy, what you avoid, and what may hold you back.

As you explore potential careers or directions, don't limit yourself. Write down every possibility, no matter how ambitious or unconventional. This brainstorming process often reveals patterns that point toward a direction you genuinely want to pursue.

## Choosing Your Career Direction

With a clearer picture of what matters to you, you can then build a list of potential career options. When creating a list, consider questions such as:

- What work have I enjoyed most so far?
- What tasks or environments do I want to avoid?
- What strengths do others frequently acknowledge?

- Do I prefer to lead, collaborate, or work independently?
- What achievements am I most proud of, and why?
- Which interests or passions could translate into a career path?

Think as big as possible first, so as not to limit your possibilities. You might explore roles that use your current skills, stretch your abilities, or even push you into a completely different field. As you narrow your options, weigh factors such as salary, location, flexibility, advancement, and work-life balance. Something that seems ideal in theory may lose appeal when compared side by side with other options.

Above all, give yourself permission to choose a path that aligns with who you are. Unique goals are valid. Some people want to lead teams; others want work-life balance or subject-matter expertise. Success is not one-size-fits-all.

Career aspirations can include:

- Increasing your salary
- Becoming a leader
- Building your network
- Traveling globally
- Earning a degree
- Improving work–life balance
- Becoming an expert in your field
- Changing careers
- Starting a business
- Writing a book

Your aspirations can be big or small, traditional or completely unique. What matters is that they feel meaningful and motivating to **you**.

## Turning Your Vision into Goals

Once your vision becomes clearer, begin identifying long-term and short-term goals that support it. Goals keep you focused, accountable, and motivated. They turn abstract ideas into concrete actions.

## Long-Term Goals

Long-term goals typically span five to ten years and represent major milestones. Because of their scope, long-term goals often fall into three categories:

- **Professional development:** building skills or earning credentials
- **Role advancement:** moving into more senior or varied roles
- **Leadership development:** strengthening communication, influence, and decision-making

Examples of long-term goals include:

- Moving into leadership
- Becoming an expert in your field
- Completing a degree or certification
- Transitioning into a new industry
- Increasing your earning potential
- Launching a business

Long-term goals require time, planning, and multiple steps. Because life changes, review these goals regularly and adjust as needed.

## Short-Term Goals

Short-term goals are the smaller steps that move you toward your long-term direction. They should be achievable within 12 months and realistic for your current stage. When goals are too ambitious, they can become discouraging. While goals that are achievable help build confidence and maintain momentum.

Examples of short-term goals include:

- Updating your resume
- Completing a course
- Attending a conference
- Meeting with a mentor
- Applying for a specialized role

- Improving a skill like public speaking or Excel

Short-term goals keep you moving forward even when your long-term vision feels far away. Break goals down as much as needed. If a long-term ambition feels distant, working backward can clarify the immediate steps required. Always frame goals positively and make them specific.

## Using the SMART Framework

To ensure your goals are clear and achievable, apply the SMART method:

- **Specific** – Define exactly what you want to achieve
- **Measurable** – Track progress with tangible milestones
- **Achievable** – Ensure it is realistic based on your resources
- **Relevant** – Confirm it aligns with your broader career vision
- **Time-bound** – Set a clear deadline

Setting SMART goals increases your likelihood of success and prevents vague intentions from stalling your progress.

# Creating Your Career Roadmap

With your goals in place, you can now build a roadmap, a practical, structured plan that helps you move from where you are today to where you want to be.

Your roadmap should include:

- A clear destination (your long-term goal)
- The key milestones along the way
- The skills, experience, or resources you need
- A realistic timeline
- A process for reviewing and updating your plan

Think of your roadmap as a living document. It gives structure, but it also adapts as your aspirations evolve or your circumstances shift.

## Assess Where You Are

Start by honestly evaluating your current skills, experience, and qualifications. Identify:

- Strengths
- Weaknesses
- Gaps between where you are and where you want to go

Feedback from trusted colleagues or mentors can help you see yourself more clearly.

Ask yourself:

- What skills do I already have?
- What skills do I need to develop?
- What experiences or certifications will move me forward?
- Which areas need improvement before I can progress?

This assessment forms the foundation of your roadmap.

## Mapping Your Path Forward

Once you understand your starting point and destination, outline the major steps required to get there. These may include:

- Enrolling in training or certification
- Gaining experience in a new role or department
- Finding a mentor
- Expanding your network
- Building leadership or communication skills
- Taking on stretch assignments

Break these into smaller, manageable actions that fit naturally within your daily life and workload.

## Choosing a Format

Writing your career plan down helps reinforce your commitment to it. A documented plan serves as a reference point, a reminder, and a tool for accountability as your career evolves.

Your roadmap can live anywhere. Depending on your preference it can be in:

- a notebook
- a spreadsheet
- a whiteboard
- a digital tool like Trello or Notion, or
- a simple document you can easily update

What matters most is consistency. Make it easy to reference, revise, and track.

## Taking Action and Tracking Progress

With your roadmap created, begin working through your steps one at a time. Track progress in a way that keeps you motivated:

- Checklists
- Progress bars
- Monthly reviews
- Note-taking
- Discussions with a mentor
- Reflection journals

Regular check-ins help you stay accountable and recognize how far you've come.

# Celebrating Milestones

It is important not to forget that acknowledging progress is just as important as making it. A milestone reached is proof that momentum is building and all your effort and hard work is paying off.

So, be sure to take the time to acknowledge and celebrate your wins, big or small. Celebrations will help boost your confidence and replenish your motivation, especially when the journey feels long or challenging.

## Reviewing and Adjusting Your Roadmap

Your roadmap is a living document and should evolve with you. To ensure it stays up to date, take the time to review it every six months and ask:

- Have my goals changed?
- Do I still want the same destination?
- Are new opportunities available?
- Do I need new skills or experiences?
- Has my timeline shifted?

Life changes, industries shift, companies reorganize, priorities evolve. It's also important to remain aware of market realities. Loyalty to a single employer doesn't always result in financial growth, particularly early in a career. Strategic job changes, when done thoughtfully, can speed up learning and compensation. However, economic conditions matter, so being flexible and open to adapting your plan if needed is key.

Goals themselves may also change over time, and that's to be expected. Revisiting your plan regularly allows you to adjust it intentionally rather than react impulsively. It can also be helpful to track any changes you make, so you can look back and see how your thinking and priorities evolved.

### When Goals Are Still Unclear

If you aren't sure what you want yet, you can use your roadmap to help focus on exploration rather than outcomes. For example, you might explore:

- New tasks
- Skill-building
- Informational interviews
- Volunteering for different projects

- Job shadowing
- Online courses in potential areas of interest

Learning what you don't want is just as valuable as discovering what you do.

## Bringing It All Together

Understanding your career vision will help give you clarity. A career roadmap connects your long-term aspirations with practical, achievable steps, helping you move forward with intention rather than guesswork. Remember:

Your career vision sets the direction.

Your goals build the structure.

Your roadmap creates the path.

By combining all three, you create a personalized, adaptable plan that keeps you focused, motivated, and moving forward, regardless of where you're starting or how your destination may evolve.

"*The Capacity to Learn Is a Gift;*
*The Ability to Learn Is a Skill;*
*The Willingness to Learn Is a Choice.*"

— **Brian Herbert**

# 3

# Developing a Growth Mindset

Once you've found a job in your ideal area, it's natural to want to settle in and relax. You did the hard work; searched for the role, passed the interview, navigated onboarding, and established yourself in the role. Routine begins to form, confidence grows and comfort follows. You deserve a breather. But this is also the moment to revisit your goals and look ahead. Delaying preparation for your next step can leave you vulnerable if unexpected changes impact your role or your team.

As you become more established, others may ask you to take on additional responsibilities. In the short term, this can be beneficial, offering exposure to new areas and helping you build experience. But without recognition, planning, or appropriate compensation, these expanded duties can become a one-sided arrangement that benefits the company more than your long-term career. Over time, you can become stuck in a role that has grown in scope without growing in title, pay, or opportunities.

Loyalty matters, but a company's priorities do not always align with an individual employee's growth. Most organizations keep employees at the level that best serves business needs, even if that means increasing responsibilities without adjusting level or salary. Companies often find it faster and more cost-effective to hire externally rather than develop someone internally, even a top performer, when they need change. This is why your development must remain a priority. No one will protect your career with the same care, intention, or urgency as you will.

Treat your career the way a business treats its strategy. Step back periodically, at least annually, to assess your current situation, identify gaps, and adjust. Decisions made in haste, or roles accepted solely to resolve immediate pressures, can unintentionally derail your long-term plans. You cannot eliminate every risk, but awareness and thoughtful planning can help reduce your exposure.

You're in a powerful position if you are confident and comfortable in your role and a sudden change wouldn't disrupt your life. If not, you should probably look at your career plan again. If you feel you've reached the top of your current career path, take time to reflect and consider new goals. If you're still progressing, map out what comes next. Ask yourself whether your plan still aligns with your priorities or whether your experiences have reshaped your direction.

Growth requires intention. Whether you have a clear vision of your next step or are still defining it, you can create momentum through habits and skills that support long-term development. Think of your career as a project. Look back at what brought you here. What worked well? What didn't? What patterns can you learn from? Reflection prevents repeated mistakes and helps you move forward with greater clarity and confidence.

## Continuous Learning

Continuous learning is the ongoing process of building knowledge, skills, and experience throughout your career. Education doesn't end with formal schooling. Every workshop, webinar, conference, article or professional interaction provides an opportunity to learn and improve. By committing to continuous learning, your skills remain relevant and adaptable and ready for the evolving workplace. In a 2021 Amazon and Gallup survey of over 15,000

U.S. adults, approximately 57 percent of workers reported being very or extremely interested in training to upgrade or learn new skills.

Continuous learning falls into three primary approaches: formal learning, social learning, and self-directed learning.

- **Formal learning** involves structured instruction delivered in a classroom or virtual environment. Many employers offer programs for job-specific skills, onboarding new employees, or leadership development.
- **Social learning** occurs through interaction with others. This includes peer-to-peer learning, mentorship, job shadowing, and day-to-day collaboration.
- **Self-directed learning** happens when individuals seek knowledge independently. This may include reading articles, listening to podcasts, watching presentations, or taking online courses. Self-directed learning is especially valuable for developing specialized skills or exploring alternative career paths.

A growth mindset is not just about learning more; it's about staying open to learning differently. The workplace evolves quickly, and adaptability is now a core skill. Continuous learning supports both technical skills, like software proficiency or project management, and soft skills such as communication, conflict resolution, networking, and presentation. Studies consistently show that soft skills have a greater influence on long-term career success than technical expertise.

Learning outside of work can take many forms, including podcasts, online courses, professional reading, and networking. Approach each experience with an open mindset. Even if a course or event isn't a perfect fit, aim to walk away with at least a few actionable insights. This mindset strengthens engagement and helps you evaluate what is most useful.

Not long ago, video conferencing was rare; now it is a workplace essential. This shift illustrates how quickly practical skills can become mandatory.

When evaluating your development, consider both technical and interpersonal capabilities. Technical skills help perform your job, while soft skills shape your reputation, relationships, and advancement potential.

Once you establish your current skill level, you build a baseline for your next phase of growth. Take advantage of employer-provided opportunities, when possible, especially those aligned with future goals. External courses, workshops, and community college programs can supplement your learning.

Stay focused on your long-term objectives when selecting learning opportunities. Ask yourself whether you are deepening your existing skills or building new ones. Keep a detailed record of courses, certifications, and development activities. While not all of them belong on your resume, maintaining documentation helps you track progress and show initiative during reviews or interviews.

For some, the idea of continuous learning may feel daunting. But this is learning you choose, learning that is relevant, practical, and aligned with your goals. Without ongoing development, skills can quickly become outdated, increasing the risk of stagnation or career vulnerability. Just as businesses evolve to remain competitive, individuals must evolve as well.

In the 2021 Amazon–Gallup poll, nearly three in four workers who pursued upskilling reported increased job satisfaction. Upskilling was also associated with an average annual wage increase of approximately $8,000. In a 2024 Built In article, ServiceNow's senior vice president of global education, Amy Regan Morehouse, described continuous learning as "a mindset—an openness to learning new things."

## Benefits of Continuous Learning

Continuous learning benefits both organizations and individuals. For employers, it builds internal talent, strengthens retention and supports adaptation to industry change. For individuals, it enhances career mobility, confidence, and long-term employability. Research from ServiceNow and Pearson projects that millions of U.S. jobs will require reskilling or upskilling in response to technological change and AI-driven shifts.

As Jay Fortuna, vice president of learning and organizational development at GoHealth, noted, growth requires evolution. Remaining static increases the risk of falling behind.

Employees consistently express a desire for skill development. A 2023 edX study reported that over 80 percent of employees view their employers as post-secondary education providers. Many also state they would stay longer at organizations that invest in learning and development.

Continuous learning is ultimately an investment in yourself. While organizations benefit from employee growth, individuals must take ownership of tracking progress and accomplishments. Keeping records of completed courses, certifications, and projects ensures people recognize your efforts, especially during performance reviews or career transitions.

Managing your career like a business means dedicating time, resources, and attention to its growth. That includes revisiting priorities, adjusting strategy when necessary, and evaluating alignment with your long-term goals. If your employer offers education support, plan and propose learning opportunities thoughtfully. Preparation makes it more likely you will get approval because employers often set budgets in advance.

## Developing and Sustaining Momentum

Continuous learning keeps you competitive, confident, and adaptable. Whether you seek advancement within your current organization or future opportunities elsewhere, relevant skills give you flexibility and confidence.

Tracking your progress is just as important as acquiring skills. Document milestones, challenges, and lessons learned. Regular reflection helps identify patterns, refine your approach, and strengthen commitment to your development.

A growth mindset isn't about constant pressure or perfection. It's about curiosity, adaptability, and steady progress. Mistakes are part of learning. What matters is how you respond, what you take from the experience, and how you move forward with intention.

By committing to growth and ongoing learning, you position yourself to navigate change thoughtfully and build a career that evolves with you and that aligns with your goals, reflects your strengths, and prepares you for whatever comes next.

"

*"Good Communication Is the
Bridge Between Confusion and Clarity."*

**— Nat Turner**

"

# 4

# Communication Essentials

Alongside upgrading your knowledge through continuous learning, another critical driver of career growth is communication. Many careers stall because people don't communicate great ideas clearly, present them confidently, or receive them effectively.

Communication is an often-underestimated skill. People often think that experience will naturally improve their communication skills, but a lack of such skills can cause them to miss opportunities or be misunderstood in their roles. Even with deep technical knowledge, you lose impact if you cannot explain your ideas clearly, discuss them thoughtfully, or share them with confidence.

Communication is not just about speaking well. It includes active listening, navigating tough conversations, presenting to groups, and adapting your message to different audiences. At its core, effective communication relies on clarity, empathy, emotional intelligence, and adaptability.

Trust sits at the center of all effective communication. People may question or dismiss messages, even simple ones, without trust. Your word choice, transparency, and tone all influence whether others trust your judgment and intentions.

Simple, intentional language can make a significant difference. For example:

- **"Here's what I know, and here's what I'm still figuring out."**
  This shows honesty and transparency, helping others rely on what you say.
- **"I want to make sure you have all the facts before making a decision."**
  This signals that you care about the person, not just the outcome.
- **"Take your time."**
  Patience and respect help others feel safe in the conversation.

These behaviors help you communicate like a leader, regardless of your title.

## Core Communication Skills

Strong communication is built on several key components:

### Clarity and Conciseness

Use simple and direct language to avoid confusion. Unless your audience understands technical jargon, avoid it and, even then, briefly define it to ensure everyone is aligned even if you use it. Speak using your natural rhythm and voice; trying to sound different often increases anxiety.

Before speaking or writing, organize your thoughts. Even a few shorthand notes can help you communicate clearly and confidently.

### Active Listening

Give your full attention to the speaker without interrupting. Show engagement through eye contact, nodding, and brief verbal cues. Paraphrasing or repeating key points helps confirm understanding and demonstrate respect.

### Nonverbal Communication

Communication goes beyond words. Body language, facial expressions, posture, and tone of voice all convey meaning. Maintain an open posture and eye contact. Always be mindful of cultural differences in gestures and physical cues.

## Empathy and Emotional Intelligence

Recognizing and respecting others' emotions helps build connection and trust. Respond thoughtfully rather than reactively and show genuine care for other perspectives.

## Confidence

Confidence builds credibility, but it should never cross into arrogance. If you feel nervous, practice conversations or presentations in advance. Nervousness often means you care, and it is common. Advanced preparation can help keep nerves from becoming overwhelming.

## Adaptability

Adjust your communication style to suit your audience. Some situations require a formal tone, while others benefit from a more conversational approach. Flexibility is a hallmark of effective communicators.

## Feedback Skills

Giving and receiving feedback can be uncomfortable, but it is essential for growth.

- Provide feedback that is specific, constructive, and respectful.
- Receive feedback with openness rather than defensiveness.

Viewed correctly, feedback becomes a powerful tool for career development.

## Digital Etiquette

Digital communication is now routine, but professionalism still matters. Be mindful of tone, clarity, and boundaries in emails, messages, and collaboration platforms. Remember that digital communications can be saved, forwarded, or reviewed later. Keep business and personal communication separate and appropriate.

# Presentation Skills

In many careers, strong presentation skills are invaluable. Presenting is not just about speaking loudly enough to be heard; technology can handle that. It's about delivering information clearly while keeping your audience engaged, whether your presentation is five minutes or two hours.

## Preparation Matters

You can never start preparing a presentation too early. Waiting too long often results in a rushed presentation and an unpolished delivery. Set internal deadlines for drafting and completing content, and rehearsing. Planning rehearsal time is just as important as preparing the material itself.

## Design Slides for Impact

Keep slides simple and uncluttered. One idea per slide works best. Use visuals, charts, images, and icons, to support your message. Choose clean fonts, consistent colors, and readable font sizes.

Always proofread your slides and, if possible, ask someone else to review them. Typos and errors can distract your audience and undermine credibility.

## Structure Your Content

Organize your presentation logically. For example, start with the problem, followed by the solution, and end with the conclusion. Walk your audience through your thinking. Avoid both extremes: too much content can overwhelm, while too little can appear shallow. Remove anything that doesn't support your main point.

End with a clear summary or call to action. This is what your audience is most likely to remember.

## Engage Your Audience

Audience involvement keeps attention high. Ask questions, use polls, or invite a show of hands. Make eye contact and rotate your focus around the room. Holding one complete thought with one person before moving on can build a connection with your audience.

A lot of unnecessary movement can be a distraction. Avoid pacing, rocking, or fidgeting. When in doubt, plant your feet, relax your shoulders, and open your posture.

Humor and storytelling can help build connection, but they should always be appropriate for the audience and setting. Authenticity matters, so be the same person when you present as when you are in the audience.

## Polish Your Delivery

Rehearse until transitions feel natural. At a minimum, practice your opening, starting strong sets the tone for everything that follows.

Vary your pace, tone, and volume to maintain interest. Avoid monotone delivery. Pause when needed. Aim to finish slightly early to give your message room to land.

## Use Technology Wisely

Use software tools to improve design, but don't overuse animations. Always have a backup plan, PDFs, printed notes, or offline copies, in case of technical issues.

## Ending a Presentation

Your ending is your last impression. Avoid ending only with a Q&A, as how your audience feels about the entire presentation will depend on the last question. If you include Q&A, weave it throughout or close with a strong final statement.

# Communication Over Video Conferencing

Strong video communication requires preparation, professionalism, and engagement.

## Tips for Better Video Conferencing

### Prepare Your Technology
Test your camera, microphone, and internet connection. Make sure you have a backup and keep software updated.

### Set the Scene
Place lighting in front of you, keep your background tidy, and position the camera at eye level.

### Communicate Professionally
Dress appropriately, speak clearly, and mute when not speaking.

### Engage Actively
Look at the camera to simulate eye contact. Sit upright, use open gestures, and acknowledge others' contributions.

### Organize the Meeting
Share an agenda in advance, start and end on time, and summarize key points and action items afterward.

### Etiquette and Respect
Avoid multitasking. Stay present. Invite quieter participants to contribute and maintain a respectful, professional tone.

# Developing Public Speaking Skills

Public speaking can be daunting, but nervousness is natural. Organizations such as Toastmasters International, the National Speakers Association, and local groups like Speak Up Club offer valuable opportunities to build confidence. Online platforms such as TED Talks and communication-focused creators (like Vinh Giang, @askvinh) also provide useful insights.

Strong communication isn't about being perfect, it's about clarity, connection, and consistency. When you invest in these skills, you strengthen not only your career growth, but also your leadership presence and professional relationships.

"

*"The Secret of Getting Ahead Is Getting Started."*

— **Mark Twain**

"

# 5

# Laying the Foundation for Career Growth

Beyond technical and communication skills, long-term career growth depends on a broader foundation. Attributes such as strong connections, motivation, and a solid work ethic play a critical role in shaping your professional trajectory.

Connections are not just limited to business contacts. They include mentors, recruiters, advisors, and peers. To borrow an old saying: it takes a village to raise a child, and it takes a network to build a career. Career growth and personal growth reinforce each other, creating a cycle of continuous improvement.

Some opportunities are obvious and impossible to miss. Others require preparation, positioning, and attention when they appear. A career takes time to build, just like Rome wasn't built in a day. Think long-term, break goals into manageable steps, and regularly refer to your career plan to ensure you're on track. By focusing on progress rather than speed, each step becomes part of the journey. The best way to predict the future is to build it.

# Networking

Networking is invaluable for career growth. As your network grows, so does your exposure to opportunities. Even if you're just starting out, begin building your network early; you never know when it will become useful.

Take advantage of professional meetings, conferences, and industry events to meet new people and learn about their career paths. You may meet an ally, someone who helps you take your first step up the ladder, or someone who introduces you to the right person.

Your network is a living system that needs care and attention. Nurture it by reconnecting periodically. This doesn't need to happen weekly or even monthly, just be intentional about it. Networking often starts slowly with simple conversations, but over time, those interactions can evolve into meaningful professional relationships. Treat all business interactions with professionalism and respect. First impressions matter, and one misstep can derail your progress. Present yourself as the professional you aspire to be.

If networking feels intimidating, start small. Say hello. Join a small group. Introduce yourself and ask others about their work. Prepare a short elevator pitch about what you do and practice it until it feels natural. Networking isn't optional, if you're not building relationships, you're missing opportunities.

# Professional Reputation

There will be moments when you need to say no — whether to protect your focus or because an opportunity simply isn't the right fit. When you do, avoid burning bridges. Careers are more interconnected than they seem, and people move, talk, and cross paths again. Treat every interaction as part of your learning journey and move forward with grace.

A resume may open the door, but your reputation keeps it open. Even the strongest resume can't outweigh a poor attitude, so show up consistently, reliably and professionally. If an opportunity doesn't work out, treat it as experience and move forward with grace.

Treat everyone with respect, regardless of their position, as careers evolve, and people rise. When managers and colleagues trust you to deliver, they're far more likely to champion your growth.

## Work Competence

Very few people rise in their careers without truly understanding their work. Learn your role thoroughly, even when the tasks feel routine. Do them well and take pride in the quality of work you deliver.

Focus on working smarter, not just harder. Strategy always outperforms sheer effort. Look for ways to improve efficiency and streamline processes, as this shows critical thinking and signals potential beyond your current position.

Aim to operate at the level of the role you want, but never at the expense of the responsibilities you're paid to perform. Master the fundamentals before taking on additional work. Falling behind doesn't impress anyone, including yourself.

Key traits that support long-term growth include:

- Willingness to learn
- Ambition and drive
- Growth mindset
- Work ethics
- Emotional intelligence

Be so good they can't ignore you.

## Communicating Complex Ideas Simply

The ability to break down complex ideas into simple, clear language is rare, and incredibly valuable. It allows you to act as a bridge between technical teams and leadership.

Practice explaining your work to people outside your industry. Strip away jargon and describe concepts as you would to a young child, without being patronized. Clarity is a powerful form of influence.

## Habits of High Performers

High achievers don't wait to feel motivated; they begin. Try committing to a task for just five minutes, and momentum often takes care of the rest.

Other habits of top performers include:

- Setting boundaries with technology to minimize distractions
- Treating important tasks as non-negotiable calendar appointments
- Applying the 80/20 rule, focus on high-impact work
- Prioritizing effectiveness over perfection
- Finishing small tasks quickly reduces mental clutter
- Focusing on execution, not just planning
- Identifying the single most important task each day

Being busy isn't the same as being effective.

## Motivation and Focus

Motivation fuels growth. Whether it comes from responsibility, recognition, financial goals, or the desire for mastery, the right motivation pushes you to keep learning and challenging yourself.

Learn to say no to distractions and yes to opportunities that support your development. Taking on extra work can showcase your capability but be thoughtful about it to never compromise your core responsibilities. If additional tasks affect your performance, clarify expectations with your manager.

Stay mindful of colleagues who shift work onto others to elevate themselves. While helping is valuable, being exploited is not. Ask whether the extra work benefits everyone or simply adds to your workload while advancing someone else.

## Staying Visible

Your manager needs to understand the work you're doing. Extra effort has little impact if it goes unnoticed. Contributing behind the scenes has value, but visibility is essential for advancement.

If someone takes credit for your work, address it professionally, either directly or through a conversation with your manager. If recognition repeatedly falls through the cracks, it may be worth reassessing the environment or its leadership.

Hard work without visibility can stall your career. As a guideline, for every ten hours of work, spend one hour ensuring the right people are aware of your results. In times of uncertainty, visibility becomes even more important; leadership often emerges in moments of challenge.

## Office Politics

Hard work alone doesn't guarantee carer progression. Politics, timing, and relationships all play a role.

Protect confidentiality. In environments where gossip spreads easily, trustworthiness becomes a rare and valuable asset. Be the person others can rely on. Refrain from sharing information that others could misuse and learn to redirect conversations tactfully and professionally.

## Leadership Skills

Leadership is not the same as management. True leadership is shown through problem-solving, initiative, and the ability to influence others.

Bring solutions, not just observations. Take initiative without overstepping boundaries. Find the balance between being proactive and being pushy. Start by volunteering for smaller responsibilities, respecting the limits of your role, and presenting thoughtful options rather than issuing directives.

## Feedback and Growth

Constructive feedback is a powerful tool for development, but not all feedback is objective. Approach criticism thoughtfully. Pause before responding, write down what you've heard, reflect on it, and seek perspective from trusted peers when needed.

Growth is not only about building skills but also about choosing direction. Confidence grows with competence. Promotions are not the sole indicator of progress. Career growth can mean expanding your skill set, taking on meaningful projects, increasing responsibility, or improving work-life balance. Not everyone aspires to management, and lateral growth can be equally valuable.

## Job Changes and Career Strategy

Corporate loyalty often yields modest returns. The most significant gains in salary and skill development often come from strategic moves between companies. Always assess new opportunities, stay confident, and look for roles where you meet about 60% of the requirements, because you can learn the rest. You may never feel completely ready for major opportunities but remember someone less qualified yet more confident is likely applying.

Strategic moves speed up growth far more than loyalty alone. Treat your career like a business, not a marriage. The stigma around job changes has largely faded, replaced by an emphasis on adaptability and continuous development.

Standing out often requires challenging the status quo. Identify one inefficient or broken process each month and propose a thoughtful solution, even if it creates discomfort. Working under demanding managers can build resilience and sharpen your standards. Recruiters frequently observe that candidates who thrive under tough leadership are better prepared for high-pressure roles later in their careers.

# Long-Term Career Growth

Competence, reputation, visibility, and focus can help build sustainable career growth. When you combine these with strong relationships, continuous learning, and intentional career planning, you position yourself for long-term success.

Treat your career as an ongoing project: invest in your development, monitor your progress, and adjust your strategy as needed. Celebrate milestones, learn from setbacks, and maintain the habits that distinguish top performers. With this foundation, every step forward becomes deliberate, meaningful, and aligned with your goals.

*"Your Network Is Your Net Worth."*

**– Porter Gale**

# 6

# Networking and Mentorship

Career growth rarely happens in isolation. Even the most capable professionals benefit from guidance, perspective, and access to opportunities, and those connections rarely appear by accident. Strategic networking and mentorship are essential tools for accelerating your career, navigating challenges, and making informed decisions.

## Understand the Purpose of Networking

Networking is not about collecting business cards or accumulating social media contacts. It's about building relationships that are genuinely valuable to both sides. The goal is to exchange knowledge, gain insight, and create opportunities through authentic, consistent engagement.

Ask yourself:

- Who can help me learn and grow
- Whose perspective might reveal opportunities I haven't considered
- Who can I support with my knowledge, experience, or network

# Build a Strategic Network

Not all contacts serve the same purpose. Focus on depth rather than breadth and cultivate relationships that support different aspects of your development:

- **Mentors:** Experienced professionals who guide your growth.
- **Sponsors:** Leaders who advocate for you and open doors.
- **Peers:** Colleagues who collaborate, share ideas, and offer support.

Maintain these relationships even when you don't need immediate help. Regular check-ins, sharing useful insights, and offering help build trust and credibility over time.

# Seek Mentorship Proactively

A strong mentor can speed up your learning, broaden your perspective, and help you avoid obstacles before they arise. Look for mentors both inside and outside your organization, and approach them thoughtfully:

- Be clear about what you hope to learn.
- Respect their time and expertise.
- Build a two-way relationship, mentorship should never be one-sided.

You may need multiple mentors to support different areas of growth, such as technical skills, leadership development, or industry knowledge.

# Give Back to Grow

Networking and mentorship thrive on reciprocity. Offer your insights, connections, or support whenever you can. Helping others strengthens your reputation, deepens relationships, and reinforces your own learning. Over time, you become known as someone who adds value, not someone who only seeks it.

## Leverage Digital Tools

Digital platforms can expand your reach and visibility, especially in today's connected world:

- **LinkedIn:** Engage with relevant content, share your insights, and connect with industry leaders.
- **Professional groups or forums:** Participate in discussions and demonstrate your expertise.
- **Virtual mentorship programs:** Many organizations offer structured opportunities to connect across locations.

## Common Pitfalls to Avoid

- **Transactional networking:** Only reaching out when you need something, erodes trust.
- **Neglecting follow-up:** Relationships require maintenance. A thank-you note, a quick update, or sharing resources goes a long way in keeping connections alive.
- **Overlooking internal networks:** Colleagues, managers, and cross-functional partners are just as important as external contacts.

## Small, Consistent Actions Make a Big Difference

Treat networking as regular practice. Monthly coffee chats, quarterly check-ins, or annual industry events all can contribute to long-term visibility and influence. Even small, consistent efforts can compound over time.

### Practical Actions to Start Today:

- Identify 5–10 people you want to connect with this quarter, mentors, peers, or industry contacts.
- Reach out with a thoughtful message or invitation for a brief conversation.
- Offer something of value before asking for guidance.
- Reflect on what you learn and adjust your networking strategy accordingly.

## Your Network as a Lifeline

A strong network isn't just about advancing your career; it's also a support system. Difficult conversations, workplace politics, or moments of uncertainty are easier to navigate when you have trusted colleagues, mentors, or peers to turn to. These relationships can provide perspective, guidance, and stability, which can help you make thoughtful decisions rather than reacting impulsively.

Just as you invest in your skills and visibility, investing in meaningful connections ensures you have the allies and insight to navigate your career with confidence and strategy.

"

*"The Oak Fought the Wind and Was Broken,*
*The Willow Bent When It Must and Survived."*

— **Robert Jordan**

"

# 7

# Navigating Workplace Challenges

When we begin a new role, we often carry the hope that this job will be *the one,* the job that recognizes our strengths, aligns with our ambitions, and propels us toward senior leadership or even the C-suite. That optimism is natural. Yet reality doesn't always unfold as expected.

What happens when things go off course?

How do you work with a manager who sees you as a threat rather than an asset? What if a colleague undermines your efforts, or conflict becomes unavoidable?

Navigating workplace challenges is a critical career skill. Understanding what is happening, and responding with professionalism, protects both your wellbeing and your long-term career growth.

## Poor Managers

When leadership falls short, you may find yourself managing your manager. This is more common than people think, because companies often promote people who lack the training to lead effectively.

A poor manager may struggle to provide clear directions, avoid giving feedback, or view capable employees as competition. In these situations, managing up can help. Start by understanding your manager's priorities and working style. Identify what motivates them, results, efficiency, control, and adapt your communication style accordingly.

A lack of clarity from a manager can lead to confusion and underperformance, not because of lack of ability, but because expectations were never defined. Some managers become rigid, believing their way is the only way. This often stems from insecurity, fear of change, or a lack of incentive to grow. Unfortunately, when a manager stagnates, your own development may stall as well.

## Leadership Changes

Leadership transitions can be disruptive at any level. Reporting lines shift, team dynamics change, and the strategic direction of the team or company may also change.

New leaders often feel pressure to make an immediate impact. Without understanding the organization's history, they may make decisions that create confusion or conflict. During these periods, some employees may try to gain favor by positioning themselves early.

How a new leader enters an organization matters. Leaders who seek broad input tend to be fairer over time. Those who quickly rely on a small inner circle may foster favoritism. Inexperienced leaders may feel insecure and become suspicious of employee intent, so be thoughtful in how you engage.

Schedule one-on-one time with a new manager as soon as possible. Building rapport early helps to counteract bias and makes sure people understand your contributions. First impressions are difficult to undo. Remain professional, measured, and consistent during leadership transitions.

# Identifying Toxic Workplaces

One of the most challenging situations an employee can face is a toxic workplace. Toxicity often begins at the leadership level and spreads throughout the organization. It may not be obvious at first, but over time something begins to feel off.

If you no longer look forward to work, pause and identify why. Is the issue situational, project-based, or systemic? Is it tied to one individual, or is it widespread?

Common indicators of a toxic workplace include:

- **Fear-Driven Leadership**
  Fear-based leadership discourages honesty and suppresses dissent. Speaking up becomes risky, and feedback is weaponized. Employees who raise concerns may be labeled "difficult" or "not team players," placed on performance improvement plans, or subtly warned to fall in line.

- **Constant Crisis Mode**
  Everything is treated as an emergency, keeping employees in survival mode and undermining long-term effectiveness.

- **Chronic Micromanagement**
  Trust is absent. Decisions are questioned, autonomy disappears, and confidence erodes.

- **No Room for Growth**
  Promised opportunities never materialize, leaving top performers stuck without real advancement.

- **Boundary Violations**
  Personal time is discouraged. Employees who work late are praised, while healthy boundaries are criticized.

- **"We're a Family" Culture**
  This language is used to justify unpaid overtime, blurred boundaries, and excessive loyalty, without fair compensation.

- **Favoritism**
  Rules apply selectively. Some employees receive protection, while others face scrutiny.
- **Lack of Recognition**
  Preventative work goes unnoticed, while visible problems receive attention.
- **Burnout as a Badge of Honor**
  Exhaustion is glorified, and rest is viewed as weakness.
- **High Turnover**
  Roles are constantly reposted, and leadership fails to reflect on why.

## Why Toxic Environments Exist

Most toxic workplaces stem from poor leadership, often driven by insecurity, fear, or low emotional intelligence. Threatened leaders may undermine strong employees rather than support them. Instead of addressing issues directly, they rely on hearsay or manufactured performance concerns.

This behavior reflects leadership failure, not employee inadequacy.

## What You Can Do

- Stay professional and composed. Don't let the chaos shake your confidence.
- Set boundaries respectfully:
  *"I can prioritize this, but it may delay X. How would you like me to proceed?"*
- Communicate with confidence. Use facts, not qualifiers.
- Document everything. Keep records of decisions, expectations and feedback.
- Request clarity and confirm objectives in writing.
- Observe patterns. Notice who is favored, silenced, or pushed out.
- Know when to leave. If stress consistently outweighs growth, begin planning your exit.

**A good boss:**

- Holds regular one-on-one meetings
- Trusts you to manage your time
- Provides context before difficult conversations
- Advocates for your visibility
- Offers consistent, actionable feedback

## Handling Conflict Professionally

When conflict arises, document conversations and follow up with written summaries. Remember: HR's primary role is to protect the company, not the employee. Be factual, calm, and prepared.

Manipulation often appears when someone blames you for reacting to disrespect while ignoring the behavior that caused it.

## Layoffs

Layoffs happen, for many reasons. In some cases, they are used to remove employees perceived as threats, disguised as performance issues. Unless you are prepared for legal action, it is often best to focus on preparing your next move and exiting professionally.

## Poor Work Relationships

Some working relationships cannot be repaired, no matter the effort. When collaboration becomes impossible, a lateral move can sometimes be a strategic exit.

Protect your mental health and your reputation. Staying in a toxic environment for too long can erode confidence, stall growth, and derail your career.

## The Bigger Picture

Workplace challenges are inevitable, but they do not have to derail your career. Learning to recognize unhealthy patterns, respond professionally, and make strategic decisions protects both your confidence and your future.

Not every job is meant to last forever. Sometimes the most professional choice is knowing when to stay, when to adapt, and when to move on. When navigated well, even difficult environments can strengthen your judgment, resilience, and long-term career strategy.

"

*"The Culture of Any Organization Is Shaped by
the Worst Behavior the Leader Is Willing to Tolerate."*

— **Gruenter & Whitaker**

# 8

## Caution -
## Toxic Manager Ahead

A t some point in nearly every career, you will encounter a toxic manager. The saying *"people don't leave jobs, they leave managers"* exists for a reason. Under toxic leadership, the impact extends far beyond day-to-day frustrations. Over time, it can erode your confidence, affect your mental health, and diminish your overall well-being. Instead of feeling engaged in your work, you may withdraw, feel anxious, or dread the workday because of constant tension or negativity.

Understanding what a toxic manager is, and how to navigate the situation when leaving isn't immediately possible, is essential for protecting both your career and your sense of self.

### What Is a Toxic Manager?

A toxic manager is someone whose repeated behaviors demoralize, control, or undermine the people they lead. Over time, these behaviors erode trust, engagement, autonomy, and a purpose, the core ingredients of a healthy work environment.

Leadership expert Peter Ronayne notes that *"Toxic bosses pull all the levers that lead to burnout."* Research supports this view. Gallup's *State of the Global Workplace* report found that many employees experience high levels of stress, worry, sadness, and anger during the workday, emotions strongly linked to poor management.

The report identified five primary contributors to burnout:

- Unfair treatment
- Unmanageable workloads
- Unclear communication
- Lack of managerial support
- Unreasonable time pressure

All five share one common factor: your manager.

## Common Signs of a Toxic Manager

A toxic manager may display one or more of the following behaviors:

- **Poor listening.** Instructions are vague, feedback is minimal, and your input is ignored or dismissed.
- **Micromanagement.** They control every detail and avoid accountability when things go wrong.
- **Public criticism.** Feedback is delivered in front of others, often in a demeaning way.
- **Unrealistic expectations.** Constant urgency and impossible deadlines without adequate resources.
- **Favoritism.** Rules apply selectively; advancement depends on proximity, not performance.
- **Credit stealing and blame shifting.** Success is theirs; failures are yours.
- **Inconsistent behavior.** They impress senior leaders but behave differently behind closed doors.

- **Emotional volatility.** Mood swings or outbursts that keep the team on edge.
- **Lack of recognition.** Hard work goes unnoticed, leading to disengagement and burnout.

Over time, these behaviors create fear, silence, and exhaustion within teams.

## Narcissistic and Insecure Managers

Some toxic managers display narcissistic or deeply insecure traits. Confident leaders do not need to declare themselves irreplaceable. Statements like *"You'll never find anyone better than me"* often signal insecurity, not strength.

These managers may:

- Resist change unless it benefits them personally
- Seek validation rather than improvement
- Feel threatened when questioned
- Prefer followers to independent thinkers

They may gaslight employees ("You're imagining things"), provoke reactions, or demand excessive explanations. The goal is often control, not clarity.

**When dealing with this behavior:**

- Stay calm, brief, and factual
- Avoid emotional or defensive responses
- Set boundaries without over-explaining
- Use silence strategically when baited

Internally labeling inappropriate behavior can help you detach emotionally and respond with intention rather than reaction.

## Why Toxic Managers Exist

Most toxic managers are not intentionally harmful. More often, they are driven by fear, insecurity, lack of emotional intelligence, or inexperience. Instead of developing their leadership skills, they protect themselves by undermining others.

Rather than taking responsibility, they deflect blame, rewrite narratives, and document situations in ways that make them appear competent while positioning others as the problem.

This is a leadership failure, not a reflection of your worth or ability.

## How to Deal with a Toxic Manager Strategically

When leaving isn't an immediate option, it's essential to think strategically rather than emotionally. Power struggles rarely lead to resolution and often escalate the situation.

**Practical strategies include:**

- **Document everything.** Follow up verbal conversations with written summaries.
- **Seek clarity**. Ambiguity often serves as a weapon.
- **Choose battles wisely.** Not every issue requires confrontation.
- **Match their communication style.** Adapt to email, verbal updates, or structured reports.
- **Build credibility elsewhere.** Strengthen relationships beyond their direct influence.
- **Regulate your emotional response.** Toxic managers often feed on reactions.
- **Limit exposure.** Reduce unnecessary interactions to protect your mental health.

If toxicity stems from insecurity, calm professionalism may reduce the perceived threat, but do not expect a toxic manager to transform.

## Protecting Yourself

Do not lose sight of who you are. If you were capable and effective before, you still are, regardless of what a toxic manager may imply.

Remember:

- Leaders support their teams during difficult times
- Toxic managers assign blame and disappear
- Leaders seek understanding
- Toxic managers avoid accountability

Prolonged exposure to toxicity can erode confidence and stall career momentum. No job is worth sacrificing your mental health.

## When It's Time to Leave

While it's tempting to believe a toxic manager will change, many do not. If you consistently feel unsafe speaking up, anxious about job security, or emotionally depleted, it may be time to explore alternatives, whether that's a transfer, a new manager, or a new organization.

Toxic leadership burns people out quickly. Sometimes, the healthiest and most strategic decision is to move on.

A strong manager creates clarity, trust, and growth. A toxic one creates fear, confusion, and exhaustion. Recognize the warning signs early, protect yourself strategically, and remember: your career is bigger than one manager.

"

*"Success Is Where Preparation
and Opportunity Meet."*

**— Bobby Unser**

# 9

# Leveraging Opportunities
# for Advancement

Career advancement rarely happens by accident. More often, it results from intentional choices, thoughtful timing, and an understanding of when to step forward, and when to pause. Recognizing and leveraging the right opportunities can significantly influence both the direction and pace of your career.

Advancement is not about saying yes to everything or chasing every visible opportunity. It requires discernment: identifying which opportunities move you closer to your long-term goals and which ones, while tempting, may quietly pull you off course.

## The Role of Networking in Career Growth

Networking remains one of the most powerful drivers of long-term career advancement. As careers progress, opportunities become less visible and more relationship driven. Referrals, internal recommendations, or informal conversations often fill many roles long before a job posting appears.

Every professional relationship you build has the potential to evolve. Former colleagues may become hiring managers, advocates, or trusted connectors. Even casual relationships can resurface years later in unexpected ways.

Rather than treating networking as something reserved for job searchers, view it as an ongoing practice. Small, consistent actions, such as congratulating someone on a promotion, commenting thoughtfully on shared work, or staying loosely connected through platforms like LinkedIn, help maintain relationships without feeling transactional.

Some people find it helpful to think of their network as a personal "board of directors." This group may include former managers, trusted peers, and industry voices you respect. Not every relationship needs to be close to be valuable. Former managers often, in particular, make especially strong advisors because they understand both your strengths and your blind spots.

## Mentorship, Sponsorship, and Strategic Relationships

Rarely do people build strong careers alone. Mentors and sponsors play different but complementary roles.

- **Mentors** provide perspective, advice, and context.
- **Sponsors** advocate for you when decisions are made behind closed doors.

Your support system may include people you speak with directly, as well as those you learn from indirectly through books, talks, podcasts, or professional content. The common thread is intentional learning. Staying open to guidance, especially from those who challenge your assumptions, helps you make better long-term decisions.

## Making Strategic Career Moves

Most careers involve change, but not every opportunity is worth pursuing. Strategic career moves require looking beyond immediate gains and considering long-term direction.

High-profile roles, impressive titles, or salary increases can be appealing, but if an opportunity pulls you too far from your intended path, it may create frustration or make realignment difficult later. Before accepting a role, ask whether the opportunity represents meaningful progress, a temporary detour, or a distraction.

Conversely, roles that appear to be a step-down can be strategic if they provide an entry into a desired field, offer critical experience, or position you for faster advancement later. Titles matter far less than trajectory. However, if you step back too far, returning to your previous level could be more challenging, so make these decisions carefully.

Pay cuts require similar scrutiny. If the reduction is temporary and manageable, and the role offers skills, exposure, or positioning that aligns with your long-term goals, it may be worthwhile. This differs from accepting lower pay out of necessity during periods such as layoffs, where stability becomes the priority.

## Visibility, Personal Brand, and Influence

Performance alone is rarely enough to drive advancement. You also need visibility, not to promote yourself, but to make sure people understand and recognize your contributions.

Positioning yourself as a reliable, thoughtful contributor builds trust and influence over time. This may include sharing insights, lessons learned, or industry perspectives through appropriate channels. Thought leadership does not require being loud or extroverted; it requires clarity, consistency, and intention.

Your personal brand is shaped by how you show up, how you communicate, and how others experience working with you. Over time, these impressions travel faster than any resume.

## Recognizing Leadership Readiness

Leadership readiness is less about confidence and more about mindset. Many people assume leadership begins with authority, but in reality, it begins with perspective.

If you find yourself focused primarily on tasks rather than direction, uncomfortable with silence in meetings, or waiting to feel fully ready before acting, it may simply mean you are still developing leadership muscles. Leadership requires patience, emotional regulation, and the ability to see patterns rather than react to individual problems.

Importantly, leadership is a responsibility, not a reward. The shift from execution to influence takes time and deliberate practice.

## Standing Out Without Overdoing It

Impressing your manager or leadership team does not require constant visibility or saying yes to everything. It comes from reliability, judgment, and proactive thinking.

Owning your work, communicating progress clearly, anticipating needs, and bringing solutions rather than problems signal readiness for greater responsibility. Equally important are emotional intelligence, how you respond under pressure, how you treat others, and how you handle feedback.

## Beliefs That Quietly Limit Growth

Many capable professionals remain unseen not because of a lack of skill, but because of unexamined beliefs. The idea that hard work alone guarantees recognition, that good work speaks for itself, or that leadership requires permission can all slow advancement.

Standing out is not a personality trait. It is a skill built through clarity, initiative, and consistency. Influence grows when you communicate clearly, act intentionally, and remain visible in ways that align with your values.

## Accepting Career Realities Without Becoming Cynical

Some realities are uncomfortable but important to acknowledge.

- Titles matter less than impact.
- Your manager may not always be your career mentor.
- Networks often open doors faster than applications.
- Office politics exist whether you participate or not.

Accepting these realities does not require cynicism. It requires strategy. Careers are shaped as much by relationships, timing, and perception as they are by performance.

## The Bigger Picture

Leveraging opportunities for advancement requires self-awareness, strategic thinking, and the courage to act intentionally. Not every opportunity is right, and not every setback is permanent. Progress does not come from moving quickly at all costs, but from moving deliberately in a direction aligned with your values, strengths, and long-term vision.

Growth is rarely linear, but with clarity and intention, it remains possible at every stage.

*"Success Is the Sum of Small Efforts,*
*Repeated Day in and Day Out."*

— **Robert Collier**

# 10

## Continuous Learning, Career Longevity, and Future-Proofing Your Path

Careers today are no longer linear. They evolve, pivot, stall, accelerate, and sometimes restart entirely. The professionals who thrive over the long term are not always the most naturally gifted; they are the most adaptable. They remain self-aware, curious, and intentional about their growth.

Sustaining a career that stays relevant, resilient, and aligned over time requires continuous learning, thoughtful boundaries, emotional regulation, and a willingness to think beyond the next role or promotion.

### Continuous Learning as a Career Strategy

Learning does not end once you land a role or reach a certain level. In fact, as responsibilities grow, the cost of stagnation increases. Skills that once differentiated you can quietly become outdated, and expertise that isn't refreshed loses influence.

Certifications and advanced education become powerful when you pursue them with intention. The question is not whether another credential looks impressive, but whether it strengthens your credibility, prepares you for where you want to go next, or signals relevance in a changing field. When learning becomes reactive, driven by fear rather than direction, it often leads to effort without impact. The most effective learning investments are those that clearly open doors.

## Staying Adaptable in a Changing Job Market

Change is no longer the exception; it is the baseline. Roles evolve, industries shift, and expectations change faster than job descriptions. What made you valuable five years ago may no longer be enough today.

Adaptability shows up in small but consistent behaviors: paying attention to industry trends, embracing new tools rather than resisting them, and remaining curious instead of defensive when change arrives. Professionals who struggle the most during transitions are often those who cling to what once worked, instead of updating how they create value.

## Strengths, Weaknesses, and Sustainable Growth

Improving weaknesses can make you more competent, but it is your strengths that create momentum. Long-term growth speeds up when your natural abilities align with what a role genuinely requires.

Understand that your "superpower" is not about ego, it's about clarity. When you understand what you do exceptionally well and place yourself in environments that reward it, growth becomes more sustainable and less forced. Weaknesses still matter, but they should not consume all your attention at the expense of what makes you distinct.

## Learning From Setbacks Without Losing Confidence

Career setbacks are uncomfortable, but they are rarely meaningless. Missed promotions, layoffs, stalled progress, or roles that turn out to be poor fits often reveal important information about skill gaps, misalignment, or boundaries that need strengthening.

The most productive response is curiosity rather than self-judgment. Instead of asking why something happened, ask what it is showing you. Setbacks often become the quiet turning points that redirect careers toward more sustainable and fulfilling paths.

## Work–Life Balance and Career Longevity

Burnout ends more careers than lack of ability. Top performers who last understand that productivity is not about constant intensity, but about managing energy over time. Sustainable careers depend on rhythm, not exhaustion.

Taking a career break or slowing momentum temporarily can look risky on paper, but when done intentionally, it often brings clarity and realignment. Choosing balance over rapid promotion may be misinterpreted by others, but it often leads people to perform well for decades instead of a few intense years. Recruiters consistently note that long-term high achievers protect their health and engagement as carefully as their resumes.

## Future-Proofing Your Career

Future-proofing does not require predicting the future perfectly; it requires paying attention. Professionals who stay relevant study where their industry is heading and position themselves slightly ahead of the curve, rather than reacting after disruption occurs.

Growth also requires questioning slow or stagnant paths. The idea that everyone must "pay their dues" for years is not universally true. Some environments grow faster than others, and some teams offer opportunities that outpace available talent. Finding and filling those gaps is often how careers accelerate.

Leadership readiness, too, is built long before the title arrives. Influence, judgment, and emotional control matter far more than hierarchy, and they are developed through experience, not promotion alone.

## Mid-Career Recalibration

Mid-career frustration is often a sign of misalignment, not failure. Priorities shift, and effort without reward becomes exhausting. Skills that once felt sharp may no longer feel future-ready.

These moments are signals to pause and reassess. Working harder is rarely the answer. Working more intentionally, revisiting direction, refreshing skills, rebuilding networks, and redefining value, usually is.

## Emotional Regulation: The Quiet Career Advantage

It takes only one poorly managed moment to damage a reputation built over years. Career success depends as much on emotional regulation as it does on intelligence or skill.

Top performers learn to pause before reacting, to reframe situations rather than personalize them, and to respond with purpose instead of release. Emotional restraint preserves credibility, influence, and optionality. Every time you choose control over reaction, you protect your long-term trajectory.

## Leadership, Habits, and Long-Term Impact

Leadership is often quiet. It shows up in consistency, judgment, accountability, and calm under pressure. It does not require being the loudest voice in the room, only the most steady and thoughtful one.

The habits that separate top performers are rarely dramatic. They protect their time, prioritize health, stay curious, communicate clearly, and execute consistently. They do not rely on motivation; they rely on discipline. Over time, these small, repeated choices compound into a meaningful advantage.

Just as importantly, they guard their reputation. Trust builds slowly and disappears quickly. People who pause before acting, take ownership, and choose integrity, even when it's inconvenient, protect an asset that no resume can replace.

## Final Reflection: Alignment Is the Goal

Career fulfillment comes from the alignment between your values and goals, your strengths and roles, and your ambition and well-being. That alignment is not a one-time decision, but a continuous process of reflection and change.

Your career is a marathon, not a sprint. Pace it wisely. Build it deliberately. And remember you can always change direction.

"*You Are Allowed to Be Both a
Masterpiece and a Work in Progress.*"

— **Sophia Bush**

# 11

## Emotional Resilience and Work-Life Integration

Career growth isn't just about capability. It's defined by durability.

Many professionals don't stall because they lack talent. They stall because they're depleted. Over time, pressure accumulates, boundaries blur, and energy erodes. The result isn't always burnout. More often, it's stagnation, working hard without momentum, performing well without progress.

Resilience allows growth to continue.

### Resilience Is a Career Skill

Emotional resilience isn't a personality trait. It's a skill built through habits, decisions, and boundaries.

Resilient professionals recover faster from setbacks. They adapt without losing confidence. They remain effective during uncertainty rather than being consumed by it. Most importantly, they protect their ability to keep going.

Resilience isn't about avoiding challenges; it's about staying strong enough to meet them.

## When Effort Stops Paying Off

Not all stress is harmful. Growth is uncomfortable by nature. But when effort no longer leads to impact, it's a signal worth noticing.

Early signs of erosion often include:

- Persistent fatigue, even when performance remains high
- Loss of motivation or creativity
- Increased irritability or emotional reactivity
- Feeling busy but ineffective

Pushing harder through these signals rarely works. Awareness comes first. Change follows.

## From Balance to Sustainability

Careers don't get balanced neatly; they integrate.

Sustainable growth comes from managing energy, not just time. It means being deliberate about where effort goes and honest about what it costs.

- **Boundaries matter.** Not every request deserves immediate availability. Protecting focus and recovery is not disengagement; it is professionalism.
- **Prioritization matters.** Not everything can be urgent. Impact outweighs volume.
- **Saying no matters.** Overcommitment doesn't signal ambition; it signals misalignment.

## Protecting the Asset: You

Your performance depends on how well you maintain the system that produces it.

Sleep, movement, nutrition, and mental recovery directly affect decision-making, emotional regulation, and focus. These aren't lifestyle extras; they are performance foundations.

Reflection is equally important. Without space to process stress, it accumulates quietly. Regular check-ins, through journaling, conversation, or professional support, prevent small strains from becoming structural problems.

Careers are not solo endeavors. Trusted peers, mentors, and networks provide perspective when your own view narrows.

## Adapting as Life Changes

Careers evolve alongside life. New responsibilities, health changes, or shifting priorities require reassessment, not guilt.

Sustainable professionals ask themselves regularly:

- What's working?
- What's draining energy?
- What needs to change?

Adjustment isn't failure. It's maintenance.

## The Long View

Unchecked stress limits careers long before it ends them. Over time, it dulls judgment, narrows opportunity, and makes movement harder.

Resilience keeps options open.

A strong career isn't built by endurance alone. It's built on pacing, awareness, and intentional choice.

## What This Means for Your Path

Your career should support your life, not compete with it. Emotional resilience isn't about slowing down; it's about staying aligned. When you protect your energy and respond to signals early, growth remains possible, sustainable, and meaningful.

Resilience doesn't just help you endure your current role; it clarifies when it's time to reassess it. Once you're no longer operating from exhaustion, fear, or constant pressure, you can evaluate your career more honestly. What once felt overwhelming becomes visible. What felt permanent becomes adjustable.

This clarity is essential, because growth isn't only about persistence; it's about knowing when to pause, reflect, and choose differently.

Work–life integration is not a final destination but an ongoing practice, one that evolves as your responsibilities, goals, and circumstances shift. The tools in this chapter help you stay grounded, aligned, and intentional, even when work and life feel demanding. But integration alone is not enough. Many professionals create strong systems and still find themselves stuck, stalled, or second-guessing their progress.

*"Knowledge Is of No Value*
*Unless You Put It into Practice."*

— **Anton Chekhov**

# 12

## Your Work-Life Integration Toolkit

Work–life integration is a foundational part of long-term career growth. It's not about achieving perfect balance; it's about creating alignment between your work, your values, and your well-being. The following toolkit provides practical exercises and reflection prompts designed to help you protect your energy, stay grounded, and make intentional choices that support both your personal life and your career. These tools can be revisited monthly, quarterly, or during times of transition to keep your life and work moving in the same direction.

### 1. Time Audit Exercise

- Track your daily activities for one week. Include work, family, personal care, and rest.
- Identify "energy boosters" and "energy drains."
- Note tasks you could delegate, streamline, or eliminate.

### 2. Priority Mapping

- List your top 5 professional priorities and top 5 personal priorities.
- Identify where they overlap and where they conflict.

- Ask yourself: Where are my non-negotiables, and where do I have healthy flexibility?

## 3. Boundary Setting Plan

- Define clear, realistic boundaries between work and personal life. Example: no emails after 7 PM, protected lunch breaks, dedicated family time.
- Track your adherence for one week and adjust where needed.

## 4. Energy Management Checklist

- Morning: What reliably energizes you? Exercise, meditation, reading?
- Midday: Are you staying focused or feeling depleted?
- Evening: What helps you unwind and reset for the next day?

## 5. Reflection Prompts

- Which tasks bring fulfillment, and which feel draining?
- Where am I overcommitting, and what can I release or renegotiate?
- What small changes could improve my overall satisfaction by 10–20%?

## 6. Weekly Alignment Review

- Spend 15–30 minutes each week reviewing whether your personal and professional priorities still align.
- Adjust schedule, commitments, or goals where needed.

## 7. Capacity Planning

Most people overestimate what they can accomplish in a week and underestimate what they can accomplish in a year.

- Identify your realistic weekly "maximum load" (meetings, work hours, personal commitments).
- Flag upcoming weeks that exceed your capacity before they begin.

- Reschedule, delegate, or decline early to protect your energy.

This prevents burnout *before* it starts.

## 8. Stress Pattern Tracking

Stress rarely occurs randomly; most people have patterns. Track:

- Times of day when stress spikes
- Situations that consistently drain or overwhelm you
- People or tasks that create tension
- Physical cues (tight shoulders, headaches, irritability)

These patterns reveal what needs boundaries, support, or restructuring.

## 9. Micro-Recovery Moments

Sustainable integration comes from small resets, not just long breaks. Examples:

- Two minutes of deep breathing
- Short walks between meetings
- Gentle stretching
- A "reset ritual" before switching tasks

These micro-recoveries support better clarity, focus and emotional regulation.

## 10. Digital Hygiene Review

Technology is one of the biggest hidden drivers of burnout.

Include:

- Notification audit (turn off non-essential alerts)
- Email boundaries (batch checking vs. constant monitoring)
- Social media time limits
- Decluttering digital spaces (desktop, files, apps)

A cleaner digital environment reduces cognitive load.

## 11. Relationship Check-In

Work–life integration is shaped by the people around you. Reflect on:

- Who energizes and supports you
- Who constantly drains you
- Who respects your boundaries
- Who disrupts them

Healthy relationships strengthen resilience, while unhealthy ones erode it.

## 12. Monthly "Life Dashboard" Review

Once a month, step back and assess the bigger picture:

- What went well
- What felt heavy
- What you want more of
- What you want less of
- What needs to shift next month

This keeps your life aligned with your values, not just your calendar.

## 13. Future Self Alignment

Keep your choices aligned with who you want to become. Ask:

- What will my future self thank me for?
- What habits support the life I want?
- What habits quietly sabotage it?

This keeps decisions grounded in long-term alignment, not short-term pressure.

# 13

# Holding Yourself Back

The greatest obstacle to your success is often not your manager, your company, or the market; it's you.

Self-doubt, distraction, fear, and hesitation quietly derail more careers than a lack of talent ever will. These forces rarely announce themselves. They appear in small decisions, delayed action, and the stories you tell yourself when things feel uncomfortable.

That's why honesty matters. Until you're willing to examine the habits, beliefs, and behaviors that hold you back, growth remains out of reach. Awareness is the first step toward change.

## The Voice in Your Head

Negative self-talk is powerful. Repeated often enough, it becomes belief.

If you constantly tell yourself you're behind, not capable enough, or not ready, your actions will reflect those thoughts. You hesitate to speak up. You delay applying. You shrink opportunities before they ever reach you.

This is why writing your goals matters. When doubt inevitably appears, your goals serve as an anchor. They remind you of why you started and what you're working toward. When discouragement surfaces, pause and look back at your progress. Growth doesn't need to be dramatic to be real. Small steps count, and they are proof that you're capable.

## "I Don't Have Time"

Everyone is busy. Time pressure is universal.

Career development doesn't require a complete overhaul of your life. One focused hour a week spent reflecting, planning, learning, or reviewing progress is often enough to create momentum. There may be periods when growth demands more time, such as training or transitions, but those investments compound, much like interest.

The story you tell yourself matters here. You're not wasting time; you're investing it.

Be realistic and be kind to yourself. Rest is essential. Burnout doesn't speed up success. Simple tools like shared family calendars, reminders, or basic project trackers can help reduce mental clutter and help you see progress clearly instead of feeling like you're constantly behind.

## "I'm Not Smart Enough"

You don't need to be a genius to succeed.

The fact that you're thinking about growth already sets you apart. Success comes in many forms, owning a business, mastering a trade, leading a team, excelling in service roles, or becoming a trusted expert. Your goal doesn't need to impress others. It needs to matter to you.

Education is not one-size-fits-all. If formal education wasn't accessible earlier in your life, that does not define your future. Take one class at a time. Ask for help. Use tutors. Explore certifications, technical paths, or trade skills. There are many roads to success, and achievement deserves celebration at every level.

## People-Pleasing and Playing Small

Being agreeable often feels safe, but it comes at a cost.

Strong professionals and leaders speak up respectfully. They don't avoid discomfort simply to keep the peace. If you regularly silence yourself, ask why. Think about the times you had a solid idea but stayed quiet, only to watch someone else voice it later and receive credit.

Even when you're wrong, owning your perspective and adjusting builds credibility. Confidence isn't about being right all the time; it's about being willing to engage.

## How People Unintentionally Sabotage Their Own Careers

**Invisibility:** One common mistake is invisibility. Doing excellent work quietly does not guarantee recognition. Results don't always speak for themselves. Keeping a simple record of wins and sharing relevant achievements ensures your contributions are seen and understood.

**Over-specialization:** Becoming "too valuable to promote" is a real risk. While expertise is important, it can become a cage. Building adjacent skills expands your mobility and opens doors instead of closing them.

**Neglecting networking:** Networking is another area where people fall behind without realizing it. Only building relationships when you need something leaves you vulnerable. One conversation a week is often enough to maintain momentum and connection.

**Underestimating your worth**: Underestimating your worth compounds quietly. Accepting below-market compensation doesn't just affect today's paycheck, it affects every future rise and opportunity. Research pay regularly. Interview occasionally, even when you're content.

**Avoiding conflict:** Peace at all costs creates limits. Difficult conversations handled early and professionally protect your growth.

Remember: you are not your first job or your last title. Try writing your ideal future role without referencing your past, then take one small step toward it.

## Visibility, Confidence, and Fear

Imposter syndrome is common, even at the top. Wondering whether you belong does not mean you don't. Confidence, not brilliance, is often what separates leaders. Own your decisions.

Visibility brings scrutiny, but it also brings opportunity. Leadership requires being seen.

Perfectionism, however, can stall momentum. Progress beats polish. "Done and delivered" will always outperform "perfect but hidden."

Feedback deserves balance, too. One critique should not erase ten positives. Learn to process input holistically rather than emotionally.

## Quiet Behaviors That Limit Growth

Some habits don't look harmful on the surface but can slowly restrict your career.

- Staying silent in meetings
- Isolating yourself
- Skipping optional events
- Saying yes to everything
- Tracking hours instead of outcomes
- Avoiding workplace dynamics entirely

Office politics exist whether or not you engage. Understanding relationships and dynamics isn't manipulation; it's a professional skill.

## Stop Giving Away Your Power

Don't wait for permission to lead.

Don't rely solely on your manager to advocate for you.

Don't confuse comfort with growth.

Don't mistake talent for leverage.

Don't avoid negotiation.

Don't hope someone will eventually notice.

Your career is your responsibility.

## Emotional Control is Power

As Warren Buffett said, *"You will continue to suffer if you have an emotional reaction to everything that is said to you."*

Restraint is strength. When words control you, others control you.

Pause. Observe. Respond with intention, not impulse.

## What Leaders Notice, Even When They Don't Say It

Leaders pay attention to consistency more than moments. They notice your attitude, how you treat others, whether you follow through, how you handle feedback and conflict, and whether you bring solutions instead of just problems.

One standout performance never outweighs weeks of reliability, or the lack of it.

## When It May Be Time to Change Direction

Chronic stress, dread of Mondays, declining confidence, ethical misalignment, exhaustion, lack of growth, or loss of meaning are not personal failures. They are signals. Ignoring them doesn't build resilience; it delays necessary change.

## Moving Forward

Don't waste your energy trying to prove yourself to the wrong audience, maintaining one-sided relationships, solving problems that aren't yours, or staying busy instead of growing.

Choose intention over fear.

Progress over perfection.

Ownership over comfort.

The moment you stop holding yourself back is the moment your career begins to move forward.

"*Change Is Inevitable.*
*Growth Is Optional.*"

— **John C. Maxwell**

# 14

# Reevaluating Your Career

Reevaluating your career is not a sign that something has gone wrong. It is a sign that you are paying attention. Careers are living things that expand, contract, shift, and evolve as you do. What once fit your identity, energy, or ambitions may no longer reflect who you've become. When life changes you, your work should have permission to change too. Stepping back to reassess is an act of self-respect. It ensures your career remains aligned with your values, strengths, and long-term direction.

## Changing Careers Later in Your Journey

Career changes later in life often carry unnecessary stigma. From the outside, it may look risky. From the inside, courage, clarity, and a refusal to settle for work that no longer feels meaningful. Your priorities at 45 or 55 are often very different from your priorities at 30, and that is growth, not inconsistency.

Many mid-career professionals report renewed motivation, better boundaries, and even greater success after pivoting. If your current role no longer reflects who you are, ask yourself one powerful question:

## What would make work feel energizing again?

A pivot doesn't always require a leap. Sometimes the next right step is consulting, project work, advisory roles, or a portfolio career that blends multiple interests. Give yourself permission to explore.

## When Effort No Longer Equals Impact

Many professionals eventually reach a point where they realize they are working harder than ever but seeing diminishing returns. Activity alone does not create value. Being busy is not the same as being effective.

This is often the moment to shift focus from tasks to impact. Clarify the difference you want to make. Move from execution into strategy and start building influence rather than simply producing output.

Impact compounds in ways effort alone never will.

## Recognizing Burnout for What It Is

Burnout rarely arrives suddenly. It shows up in patterns. You may feel overloaded, undervalued, disconnected, or stuck. In these moments, prioritization and boundaries matter far more than endurance. Burnout often stems from a loss of control when you feel like a passenger in your own role rather than the driver.

Common contributions include:

- Unclear expectations
- Constant urgency
- Toxic or negative environments
- Lack of recognition
- Too much responsibility and too little control

Speaking up, realigning expectations, setting boundaries, or seeking a healthier environment are not dramatic actions, they are protective ones. Burnout is not a test of strength. It is a signal that something needs to change.

Confusing or shifting expectations create additional strain. When success is unclear, stress becomes constant. Asking for clarity, feedback, and alignment can remove pressure that never should have been there in the first place.

Toxic cultures, persistent negativity, and poor leadership also take a cumulative toll. Staying professional while protecting your boundaries is essential, and sometimes, the healthiest decision is recognizing when its time to move on.

Other warning signs include feeling unappreciated, disconnected, insecure about job stability, or stuck in repetitive work with no room to grow. These signals are not signs of personal weakness; they are information. Ignoring them doesn't build resilience; it delays necessary change.

## Career Myths Worth Letting Go Of

Many people stay stuck because they're operating under outdated assumptions. Letting go of outdated beliefs is often the first step toward growth.

### Myth: Staying at one company equals stability.

Strategic job changes often accelerate growth, expand skills, and increase compensation. Stay as long as you're learning and advancing. When growth stops, it's time to reassess.

### Myth: Your resume must include every job.

Employers want relevance, not a biography. Highlight experiences that support where you're going next.

### Myth: The corporate ladder is the only path.

Modern careers are rarely linear. Lateral moves, pivots, entrepreneurship, and hybrid paths are often smart, intentional choices.

**Myth: Hard skills matter most.**

Communication, adaptability, emotional intelligence, and the ability to influence often determine who advances.

**Myth: Playing it safe is the safest choice.**

Calculated risks, taken thoughtfully and incrementally, often lead to the greatest rewards.

## Signs You May Be Underpaid

Being underpaid rarely announces itself clearly. More often, it shows up subtly:

- Staying in the same role for years with modest raises
- Being the "go-to" person without a title or compensation change to match
- Not knowing your market value

If your skills are current but your salary isn't, or you're performing multiple roles without multiple forms of compensation, it's time to pay attention.

Companies that describe themselves as "like family" sometimes rely on emotional loyalty instead of fair market pay. Fear of negotiation is one of the most expensive fears a professional can carry.

Remember: Loyalty doesn't pay bills. Market value does.

## Short-Term Goals Versus Long-Term Direction

Short-term goals serve as milestones, typically achievable within six months to a year. They should always support a longer-term vision. Regularly comparing the two helps ensure your daily efforts are moving you forward. Skills like leadership, negotiation, decision-making, and communication under pressure and take time to develop. Long-term thinking focuses on transferable skills rather than job titles. It helps you say no to distractions, stay flexible when plans change, and connect day-to-day work to a larger purpose.

## Building a Career Plan That Evolves with You

Start with reflection and consider:

- Where do I want to go?
- What energizes me?
- What skills do I already have?
- What skills do I need to strengthen?
- What options have I dismissed too quickly?

Then gather feedback. We are often poor judges of our own blind spots. Mentors, peers, and leaders can offer insights into behaviors to develop, skills to prioritize, and capabilities that would help you level up or pivot effectively.

## The Power of Continuous Learning

Continuous learning is one of the most reliable career accelerators available. It builds adaptability, confidence, and opportunity while opening doors to new paths.

Modern careers resemble jungle gyms more than ladders. Learning allows you to move sideways, diagonally, and upward with intention. The more you invest in yourself, the more momentum you create, and the easier growth becomes.

## The Career Accelerator Formula

**Self-worth + Clear direction + Strategic communication = momentum.**

When you believe in your value, know where you're headed, and can communicate it effectively with confidence, reevaluation stops feeling like a crisis, and starts feeling like a strategy.

# Career Decision-Making Framework

When you're considering a career change, promotion, or new opportunity, uncertainty can feel overwhelming. A structured framework brings clarity and reduces bias, helping you make intentional choices rather than reactive ones.

## 1. Assess Your Current Situation

Ask yourself:

- Am I growing in my current role? (Skills, visibility, compensation, satisfaction)
- Does my work align with my career vision?
- Are there opportunities here that will prepare me for the next step?

This step is about understanding reality, not assigning blame. It's a stock take of your career assets, gaps, and opportunities.

## 2. Define Your Goals

Clarity drives decisions. Determine:

- What do I want in the next 12–24 months?
- Which skills or experiences will move me closer to my vision?
- What does success look like personally and professionally?

Write these goals down as they become your north star.

## 3. Gather Data

Research and information are your friends. This includes:

- Market trends and emerging skills
- Salary benchmarks and benefits packages
- Company culture and leadership reputation
- Possible mentors or networks

Having accurate, objective data reduces the risk of decisions based on assumptions or fear.

## 4. Evaluate Options Against Your Goals

For each potential move, whether it's staying, changing roles, or leaving, ask:

- Does this move align with my career vision?
- Will it advance my skills, network, or visibility?
- What are the trade-offs in compensation, lifestyle, and stability?
- Does it feel challenging but achievable?

Score or rank your options if it helps clarify your choice.

## 5. Consider Risks and Mitigation

Every decision carries risk. Evaluate:

- What could go wrong?
- How can I minimize these risks?
- What is reversible vs. irreversible?

Understanding risk allows you to act confidently instead of avoiding choices out of fear.

## 6. Make the Decision and Commit

Once you've assessed, gathered data, and weighed trade-offs, make your choice.

- Decide based on evidence, goals, and personal values, not pressure or emotion.
- Outline immediate next steps to implement the decision.

## 7. Review and Adjust

Even well-informed decisions should be monitored. Set checkpoints:

- Am I seeing the expected growth?
- Are there unexpected outcomes or lessons?

- Do I need to pivot or recalibrate?

Careers are dynamic. Revisiting your decisions regularly ensures momentum and alignment with evolving goals. Careers are dynamic; your plan should be too.

**"**

*"The First Step Towards Getting Somewhere
Is to Decide You're Not Going to Stay Where You Are."*

— J.P. Morgan

# 15

## Navigating Career Transitions with Professionalism and Intention

Starting a new chapter, whether entering or exiting a role, is one of the most defining parts of your career. How you handle transitions often says more about your professionalism than the time you spent in any position. The goal isn't perfection; it's self-awareness, discipline, and thoughtful restraint.

### Moves to Avoid in a New Job

The desire to impress early is natural, but over-promising is one of the quickest ways to undermine credibility. Instead of trying to prove yourself immediately, pace yourself. Build in extra time, deliver consistently, and allow your results to speak for you. Trust grows faster through reliability than through grand gestures.

## Being Unprepared

Showing up unprepared is another early misstep that's difficult to recover from. It's usually obvious when someone is improvising. Preparation signals respect for the role, the people, and the opportunity. When others see you taking preparation seriously, they're far more willing to invest in you.

## Resisting Feedback

Being uncoachable can quietly stall your momentum. Feedback is not a personal attack; it's information. Becoming defensive shuts down learning. Focus on the core issue, take action, and communicate how you're improving. Demonstrated growth earns credibility.

## Complaining Too Early

Complaining early leaves a lasting impression, and rarely a positive one. Every workplace has flaws, but your first responsibility is to observe and understand before judging. If something truly needs improvement, offer solutions rather than complaints.

## Engaging in Gossip

Gossip is another early trap. Few things damage trust faster. If a conversation turns negative, redirect it or step away. People remember who maintains professionalism.

## Avoiding Responsibility

Avoid dodging ownership, especially when mistakes occur. Taking responsibility for both wins and missteps shows integrity. Doing the right thing, even when it's uncomfortable, builds a reputation that follows you.

### Arriving Late of Disorganized

And never underestimate punctuality. Being on time signal's reliability, respect, and discipline.

These behaviors create an impression that can take months to repair. Starting strong doesn't require brilliance; it requires steadiness.

## Mistakes to Avoid When Leaving a Job

How you leave matters just as much as how you arrive.

### Leaving Angry or Impulsively

Even if your experience was difficult or unfair, leaving with anger or rudeness only harms you. Stay calm. Exit with kindness. Your future self will benefit from the restraint.

### Disappearing Without Closure

Disappearing without saying goodbye may feel easier, but it leaves a poor impression. Even a brief message shows respect for yourself and for the time you spent there.

### Oversharing Your Reasons for Leaving

Avoid oversharing the details of your departure. While honesty is important, excessive explanations often appear unprofessional. Keep your reasoning brief and neutral. Some stories are best reserved for trusted friends.

### Leaving Disorganized Work Behind

Leaving chaos behind reflects poorly on you, not the organization. Even if the role wasn't ideal, finish strong. Organize files, leave notes and make the transition easier for the next person. Your name remains attached to the work you leave behind.

## Venting Publicly Online

Publicly venting, especially online, is one of the most damaging exit mistakes. It may feel cathartic, but future employers view it as a risk. Vent privately. Protect your reputation.

## Ghosting Meaningful Relationships

Don't ghost colleagues. Leaving a job doesn't mean leaving meaningful relationships behind. Stay connected with those you respect. Strong relationships often lead to unexpected opportunities.

Before you go, save examples of your best work within company guidelines. Projects, awards, positive feedback, and accomplishments form part of your professional narrative. You'll need them later.

And finally, acknowledge yourself. Even though the role was challenging, you made it through. Mark the transition in a small, meaningful way. You're entering a new chapter; you've earned this moment.

# Why Moving on Matters

Transitions can bring excitement, uncertainty, or both. Change is uncomfortable, but it is also where growth happens. New roles stretch your skills, expand your confidence, and expose you to new people and perspectives.

While staying put may feel safer, it often limits earning potential. The largest salary increases typically come from changing companies, not annual raises. Organizations invest more to attract new talent than to retain existing employees.

Changing companies can also make you more attractive to future employers. It signals adaptability, broader experience, and exposure to different environments. You're seen as flexible, open to learning, and capable of navigating change.

Moving on isn't about restlessness; it's about progression. When approached thoughtfully, transitions strengthen your career rather than disrupt it.

"*Growth and Comfort Do Not Coexist.*"

— **Ginni Rometty**

# 16

## Advancing Your Career

Talent rarely limits career growth. More often, progress stalls because people stop being intentional. They stay loyal in the wrong places, wait for recognition that never comes, or assume effort alone will carry them forward.

Once your career is in motion, it won't sustain momentum on its own. Careers require stewardship. You must maintain the pace by changing it and sometimes speeding it up on purpose. Opportunities rarely arrive neatly packaged, and progress is almost never announced in advance. If you wait for certainty, permission, or perfect timing, you will wait far longer than you should.

True growth comes from owning your performance and your direction. It requires nurturing momentum, recognizing when your development has paused, and taking purposeful action to keep your career moving with intention.

## Loyalty Doesn't Pay

In the past, companies rewarded long-term employee loyalty with steady promotions and job security. That model no longer exists.

Few organizations remain loyal to long-tenured employees, and this is most visible in compensation. Loyalty often results in being underpaid, receiving modest annual increases while new hires enter at higher market-aligned salaries.

To protect yourself, regularly compare your compensation to current job postings and industry benchmarks. If there is a gap, decide whether you're willing to accept it, or whether it's time to move on.

## Relevance Matters More Than Effort

Hard work is not the same as being relevant. You can be dependable, dedicated, and deeply committed, and still fall behind if your skills no longer match what the market values.

Industries evolve. Technology advances. Expectations shift. The skills that earned you credibility five years ago may already be losing value.

Staying relevant means making intentional choices to remain useful, adaptable, and in demand. Pay attention to how roles are changing, which skills appear repeatedly in job postings, and what leaders emphasize for the future. If your work hasn't evolved in a while, that's a signal, not a failure.

## Skill Development Is Career Insurance

Your skills are your most portable asset. Titles change. Companies change. Skills travel with you.

Set aside regular time, weekly or monthly, to invest in learning. This may include strengthening technical expertise, adopting new tools, or developing soft skills such as communication, decision-making, and leadership. People often underestimate soft skills, but they consistently distinguish high performers from those who plateau.

The goal is progress, not perfection. Small, consistent investments in skill development create options for future opportunities, especially when change arrives unexpectedly.

## Networking and Mentorship Are Not Optional

Career growth does not happen in isolation. Opportunities move through people long before they appear on job boards. Promotions, role changes, and new paths often begin with a conversation, not an application.

Networking isn't about self-promotion, it's about staying connected, curious, and visible. Maintain relationships even when you don't need anything. Check in with former colleagues. Congratulate people on milestones. Share insights or resources when appropriate. These small gestures build trust over time.

Mentorship adds another layer of perspective. Seek mentors both inside and outside your organization. They help you see opportunities, avoid pitfalls, and speed up your development. They also help you understand the unspoken rules of your industry and provide guidance you cannot get from books and courses alone.

## Financial Awareness Fuels Growth

Career growth isn't only about skills and visibility; it's also about understanding your financial landscape. Financial literacy is a form of self-respect and a safeguard against stagnation.

**Know your market value.** Benchmark your salary regularly against industry standards, geographic factors, and comparable roles.

**Look beyond base salary.** Compensation includes bonuses, benefits, stock options, retirement contributions, and development opportunities. A role with slightly lower pay but greater long-term potential may be a smarter investment.

**Negotiate strategically.** Negotiation is not a one-time event; it's a recurring part of career advancement. Approach these conversations with data, clarity and confidence.

**Plan financially.** Managing your income, expenses, and savings gives you the freedom to make career decisions based on growth, not fear.

## Comfort Is the Enemy of Momentum

Comfort can feel like success, but it often signals stagnation. If your role no longer challenges you, if feedback becomes repetitive, or if growth feels optional, you may be on a plateau.

Plateaus aren't failures, they're indicators that your growth has outpaced your environment.

When effort no longer leads to impact, pushing harder isn't the answer. Reassessment is. That may mean renegotiating your role, seeking new responsibilities, or exploring opportunities elsewhere. Discomfort is not something to avoid, it's something to use. Growth often feels awkward before it feels rewarding.

## Own the Story of Your Career

Your career story exists only in your mind unless you articulate it. Track your accomplishments, maintain a living record of outcomes, and be prepared to explain, not boast, what you've done, learned, and where you're headed next.

Craft a concise professional narrative for conversations, interviews, and networking moments. Clarity builds confidence, and confidence attracts opportunity.

## Moving Forward with Intention

Career growth is not about constant motion; it's about intentional motion.

- Stay aware of your relevance.
- Invest in skills that travel.

- Build and maintain relationships.
- Understand your financial worth.
- Challenge yourself before complacency sets in.

When you combine competence, visibility, adaptability, and self-awareness, growth becomes less about luck, and more about choice. And when the path you're on no longer fits, the most important skill of all is knowing when it's time to reassess.

Your career will only grow if you actively choose to grow with it.

*"Your Brand Is What People Say About
You When You're Not in the Room."*

— **Jeff Bezos**

# 17

# Personal Branding and Digital Presence

Whether you realize it or not, you already have a personal brand.

It lives in how people describe you when you're not in the room, what appears when someone searches for your name, and how consistently your skills, experience, and values show up across professional spaces. The only question is whether that brand is intentional, or accidental.

In today's career landscape, performance alone is no longer enough. Visibility matters. Narrative matters. And increasingly, your digital presence plays a direct role in how opportunities find or pass you by.

This isn't about becoming an influencer, oversharing online, or turning your career into a marketing campaign. It's about clarity, consistency, and control. A strong personal brand ensures that when opportunity appears, your professional story is already working on your behalf.

## What Personal Branding Really Means

Personal branding is not self-promotion. It is alignment.

Your brand is the intersection of:

- What you are good at
- What you are known for
- What the market values

When these three are aligned, your career moves more smoothly. When they don't, growth becomes harder than it needs to be.

A clear personal brand helps others understand where you add value, what problems you solve, and how you think. Without that clarity, people fill in the gaps themselves, and their assumptions are rarely strategic.

## Why Digital Presence Now Matters

Hiring decisions, promotions, speaking invitations, and referrals increasingly begin with a search, not a conversation.

Your LinkedIn profile, online bio, published content, or even absence online, all communicate something. Silence is not neutral. An outdated or incomplete digital presence can quietly signal stagnation, while a thoughtful one signals relevance and momentum.

This doesn't require constant posting or personal exposure. It requires accuracy, intention, and upkeep.

Think of your digital presence as your professional storefront. It doesn't need to be flashy, but it should be current, credible, and easy to understand.

# Owning Your Professional Narrative

If you don't articulate your career story, someone else will, and their version may not reflect your reality.

Your narrative should answer three questions clearly:

1. What do you do?
2. What problems do you solve?
3. Where are you headed next?

This narrative should be consistent across:

- Your resume
- Your LinkedIn profile
- Networking conversations
- Interviews and introductions

Craft both a short version (30 seconds) and a longer version (2 minutes). The goal isn't memorization, it's clarity. When your story is clear, confidence follows naturally.

# LinkedIn Is Not Optional

LinkedIn is no longer just a job-search tool. It is a living record of your professional identity.

At a minimum, your profile should:

- Reflect your current role accurately
- Highlight measurable accomplishments, not just responsibilities
- Signal the direction your career is moving, not just where it has been

Your headline should communicate value, not simply your job title. Your summary should sound like a person, not a resume. And your experience section should focus on outcomes.

You don't need to post frequently. But when you engage, sharing insights, commenting thoughtfully, or contributing to relevant discussions, you reinforce visibility and credibility.

## Consistency Builds Trust

Inconsistent messaging creates confusion.

If your resume says one thing, your LinkedIn profile says another, and your conversations tell a third story, people hesitate. Trust is built when your message aligns across platforms and over time.

Review your professional materials regularly. Ask yourself:

- Does this reflect what I actually do?
- Does it support where I want to go next?
- Does it sound current, or dated?

Consistency doesn't mean rigidity. It means coherence.

## Personal Branding Without Oversharing

Professional visibility does not require personal exposure.

You do not need to share private details, strong opinions, or your entire life online. A strong brand can be built through:

- Thoughtful insights
- Lessons learned
- Industry observations
- Professional milestones

Choose a level of visibility that feels sustainable. Authenticity matters more than volume.

## Managing Your Reputation Over Time

Your brand is shaped not only by what you say, but by how you behave.

Reliability, follow-through, professionalism, and emotional regulation all reinforce your reputation. Online and offline behavior are no longer separate. How you communicate digitally matters just as much as how you show up in meetings.

Be mindful of:

- Tone in written communication
- Public comments and interactions
- How you handle disagreement or criticism

Your reputation compounds, positively or negatively, over time.

## Visibility Supports Opportunity

Most opportunities do not arrive through formal applications. They arrive through recognition.

When people understand what you do and trust how you operate, they think of you when opportunities arise. Visibility doesn't guarantee success, but invisibility guarantees exclusion.

You don't need to be everywhere. You need to be findable, credible, and clear.

## Personal Branding Is Ongoing, not a One-Time Task

Your career will evolve. Your brand must evolve with it.

Revisit your narrative as roles change, skills grow, and priorities shift. What served you early in your career may limit you later if left unchanged.

Treat personal branding the same way you treat skill development or networking, not as a one-time effort, but as a maintenance practice.

## Bring It All Together

Personal branding is not about ego, it's about stewardship. It ensures that your work, skills, and experience are represented clearly and accurately, so when opportunity meets readiness, nothing gets lost in translation. You don't need to be louder; you need to be clearer. And in a world where careers increasingly unfold in public and digital spaces, clarity is one of the strongest tools you have. Now that your professional presence is defined and intentional, the next step is to zoom out and look at the broader principles that shape a meaningful, resilient career. Before mapping out your next moves, it helps to step back and understand the philosophy that ties all of it together.

"

*"Simplicity is the Ultimate Sophistication."*

**— Leonardo da Vinci**

"

# 18

# The Career Philosophy

Your career will rarely unfold in a straight line. It evolves through how you respond to change, the habits you build, and the decisions you make, often quietly, over long stretches of time. A fulfilling career is not something that simply happens to you. You shape it through intention, self-awareness, and the willingness to adjust when the path no longer fits.

Progress comes not from working harder, but from working with clarity. It requires being honest about where you are, deliberate about where you're going, and open to recalibrating along the way. Growth begins with ownership. No organization, mentor, or manager will ever care more about your development than you do. That truth can feel daunting, but it is also empowering, because ownership unlocks momentum.

Skills matter, but relevance matters more. What made you valuable yesterday may not carry you forward tomorrow. Continuous learning protects your adaptability and keeps you useful in a changing market. Small, consistent investments compound over time.

Relationships move careers. Opportunities often surface through trusted connections long before they become public. Visibility is not self-promotion; it is simply making the value you deliver unmistakable.

Discomfort is a signal of growth. When everything feels easy, you may have outgrown your environment. Stagnation is not always dramatic; sometimes it looks like performing well in a role that no longer stretches you. When effort no longer leads to impact, reassessment, not overwork, is the answer.

Loyalty should be mutual. Stay where you are learning, growing, and being valued. Move on when those conditions shift. Your career is a long game, and strategic movement is part of that journey.

Reputation compounds over time. Integrity, emotional regulation, follow-through, and clarity in how you communicate, shape how people experience you long before they read your resume. Protect your reputation carefully as it travels ahead of you.

While perfection is not required, attention is. Most decisions are reversible. Waiting indefinitely for certainty often creates more risk than making a thoughtful move forward. Action creates clarity, not the other way around.

Above all, alignment matters. Alignment between your strengths and your work. Between your values and your environment. Between ambition and well-being. Careers evolve, and you are allowed to evolve with them.

Your career is yours to write. Revisit it often, refine it as you grow, and move with intention. The choices you make today shape the story you tell tomorrow.

These principles form the foundation of a career built with intention and clarity. Now, let's turn them into practical steps you can apply every day

*"Surround Yourself with People*
*Who Fight for You in Rooms You Aren't In,*
*and Be That Person for Others."*

— **Simon Koerner.**

# 19

## The Career Playbook

This chapter gives you a practical roadmap for putting everything you've learned into daily, weekly, and long-term action. Think of it as a living guide, a structure you can return to at any stage of your career.

### Own Your Career

Take initiative. Track accomplishments, set goals, and communicate your value clearly. No one will champion your growth more than you.

### Clarify Your Vision

Define success on your own terms. Revisit your goals regularly as your life, priorities, and strengths evolve.

### Commit to Continuous Learning

Dedicate weekly time to learning. Stay adaptable, refresh core skills, and invest in both technical and soft-skill development.

## Build and Maintain Relationships

Nurture mentors, peers, and industry contacts. Strategic networking builds visibility, trust, and access to opportunities long before they surface.

## Understand Your Market Value

Benchmark compensation and benefits. Advocate for fair pay and make financially strategic career decisions.

## Embrace Discomfort and Seek Feedback

Growth requires stretching beyond what feels easy. Feedback is not a judgment, it's actionable information.

## Integrate Work and Life Intentionally

Set boundaries, manage energy, and check in with yourself regularly. Sustainable success requires well-being, not exhaustion.

## Protect Your Reputation

Show integrity, reliability, and professionalism consistently. Reputation is one of your strongest career assets.

## Create Career Momentum

Make strategic decisions that move you forward. Reevaluate periodically, and be willing to shift roles, teams, or organizations when growth stalls.

## Focus on Impact

Effort matters, but impact is what moves your career. Identify the work that creates meaningful outcomes, and prioritize it.

## Pursue Alignment

Career satisfaction grows where your values, strengths, and life priorities meet. Revisit alignment as your circumstances change.

## Final Perspective

Your career is a long game built on many small, intentional steps. You do not need to have everything figured out today; you simply need to keep moving forward with clarity, curiosity, and courage.

Your next step matters more than your last.

"

*"What Lies Behind Us and
What Lies Before Us Are Tiny Matters Compared
to What Lies Within Us."*

— **Ralph Waldo Emerson**

"

# Resources

*8 Signs of a toxic boss and how to deal with them (Until you can GTFO) | The Muse.* (n.d.). The Muse. https://www.themuse.com/advice/toxic-boss-signs-how-to-deal

Alliance, W. R. (2025, August 18). Achieve sustainable Work-Life Balance. *WOCRA.* https://www.wocretailalliance.org/post/strategies-for-long-term-personal-and-career-integration-and-prioritization

Alliance, W. R. (2025b, August 18). Achieve sustainable Work-Life Balance. *WOCRA.* https://www.wocretailalliance.org/post/strategies-for-long-term-personal-and-career-integration-and-prioritization

Bernuzzi, C., Sommovigo, V., & Setti, I. (2022). The role of resilience in the work-life interface: A systematic review. *Work,* 73(4), 1147–1165. https://doi.org/10.3233/wor-205023

Bishop, K. (2025, January 15). *When Switching Employment, What % Gain In Pay Is Typical?* JobsCareerHunters.com. https://jobscareerhunters.com/when-switching-employment-what-gain-in-pay-is.html

*Bot verification.* (n.d.). https://eggcellentwork.com/signs-of-a-toxic-boss/

*Career Development: definition, planning & resources.* (n.d.). Built In. https://builtin.com/career-development

Curci, M., & Curci, M. (2025, April 2). The role of Work-Life Balance in Long-Term Career Growth - Career Guidance advice. *Career Guidance Advice -.* https://careerguidanceadvice.com/the-role-of-work-life-balance-in-long-term-career-growth/

Gallup, Inc. (2021). State of the Global Workplace Report. In *Gallup.com*. https://www.gallup.com/workplace/349484/state-of-the-global-workplace-2022-report.aspx

Gallup. (2024). *Mapping the careers of the future in the United Kingdom, France and Germany.*

*How To Map a Clear Career Plan (With Example).* (2025, December 10). Indeed. https://www.indeed.com/career-advice/finding-a-job/how-to-create-career-plan-example

Iacurci, G. (2025, August 22). *Wage growth is doing something odd in 2025 — the last time it happened was around the Great Recession.* CNBC. https://www.cnbc.com/2025/08/22/wage-growth-2025-job-switcher-job-stayer.html

Ismail, S., Potgieter, I. L., & Coetzee, M. (2023). Self-regulatory employability attributes and competency: the strengthening role of grit. *Frontiers in Psychology, 14,* 1298299. https://doi.org/10.3389/fpsyg.2023.1298299

James, D. (2023, July 19). *Job vs. Career: Top Differences and Insights Between the Two.* Entrepreneur. https://www.entrepreneur.com/living/job-vs-career-top-differences-and-insights-between-the-two/455543

Job Hopping vs. Career Stability: Which is Better for Your Career? (2024, December 20). *Jobsolv.* https://www.jobsolv.com/blog/job-hopping-vs-career-stability-which-is-better-for-your-career

*Job Switch vs Internal Promotion: Which Gets You a Bigger Pay Rise.* (2025, July 1). CVlibrary. https://www.cv-library.co.uk/career-advice/latest/job-switch-vs-internal-promotion/

Jonathan Rothwell, Gallup Principal Economist and Senior Fellow at the Brookings Institution. (2021, September 9). *The American Upskilling Study shows workers want skills training.* About

Amazon. https://www.aboutamazon.com/news/workplace/the-american-upskilling-study-shows-workers-want-skills-training

Minshew, K. (2023, March 7). *Most employees say their workplaces are "toxic." What if you're the toxic one? | Fortune.* Fortune. https://fortune.com/2023/03/07/most-employees-workplaces-toxic-jobs-careers-mental-health/

Nadeem, R., & Nadeem, R. (2024, December 10). *5. Key labor force trends.* Pew Research Center. https://www.pewresearch.org/social-trends/2024/12/10/key-labor-force-trends/

Nadeem, R., & Nadeem, R. (2025, April 24). *Majority of U.S. workers changing jobs are seeing real wage gains.* Pew Research Center. https://www.pewresearch.org/social-trends/2022/07/28/majority-of-u-s-workers-changing-jobs-are-seeing-real-wage-gains/?utm_source=newsletter&utm_medium=email&utm_campaign=newsletter_axioswhatsnext&stream=science

*One third of your life is spent at work.* (n.d.). Gettysburg College. https://www.gettysburg.edu/news/stories?id=79db7b34-630c-4f49-ad32-4ab9ea48e72b

Rumage, J. (2024, April 29). *What is continuous learning and why is it important?* Built In. https://builtin.com/articles/continuous-learning

School of Professional Studies at Wake Forest University. (2025, October 19). *Self Care for Career Success: 6 Tips to Balance Work and Life - School of Professional Studies at Wake Forest University.* https://sps.wfu.edu/articles/tips-to-balance-work-and-life/

Smaliukienè, R., Bekesiene, S., & Hoskova-Mayerova, S. (2024). Editorial: Emotional resilience for wellbeing and employability: the role of learning and training. *Frontiers in Psychology, 15,* 1379696. https://doi.org/10.3389/fpsyg.2024.1379696

Striesand, B. (2023, May 27). *Reskilling in the AI era.* Workflow by ServiceNow. https://www.servicenow.com/workflow/hyperautomation-low-code/reskilling-ai-and-the-future-of-work.html

The importance of work-life balance: A comprehensive guide. (2025, June 3). *KU Business.* https://onlinemba.ku.edu/experience-ku/mba-blog/promoting-work-life-balance

Vanourek, D. (2025, February 24). *Toxic leaders destroy more than just productivity.* https://www.linkedin.com/posts/doravanourek_7-toxic-leaders-youll-meet-in-your-career-activity-7299795459047337984-gpFd/

Williams, A. (2025, August 28). *Employers are seen as the new post-secondary colleges, but can they deliver?* Business edX. https://business.edx.org/expert-insight/employers-seen-as-the-new-post-secondary-colleges-but-can-they-deliver/

# Thank You

Dear Reader,

Thank you so much for taking the time to read my book. Your support truly means the world to me. If you found value in these pages, I would be deeply grateful if you could take a moment to leave a review on Amazon or Goodreads.

Your feedback not only helps me continue growing as a writer, but it also helps other readers discover the book. Whether you share a few words or a longer reflection, your voice matters, and it makes a meaningful difference.

Warm regards,
**R. D. Bennett**

# Books by R. D. Bennett

## Career & Professional Growth

Straightforward, empowering guides for building a meaningful career, advancing with purpose, and navigating modern workplace challenges.

**A Roadmap For The Job Hunt:**

A Practical Guide to Mastering Interviews, Resumes and Landing the Job

## Menopause Spotlight Series

A practical, compassionate series designed to help women navigate perimenopause, menopause, and postmenopause with clarity, confidence, and evidence-based support.

**Menopause Spotlight**

Understanding and Managing
Brain Fog

**Menopause Spotlight**

Your Essential Guide to
Perimenopause, Menopause,
and Beyond

Helping readers learn, grow, and navigate life with clarity and confidence.

# About The Author

R. D. Bennett is a nonfiction writer based in Virginia, where she lives with her family. With a background in healthcare and leadership, she writes to inform, support, and uplift, bringing evidence-based insight and a practical, compassionate tone to every topic she explores.

www.ingramcontent.com/pod-product-compliance
Lightning Source LLC
Chambersburg PA
CBHW060615130626
46555CB00002B/522